THE LEGAL QUALITIES OF MONEY

The
LEGAL
QUALITIES
of
MONEY

by **ARTHUR KEMP**

PROFESSOR OF
MONEY AND CREDIT

Claremont Men's College
and Claremont Graduate School
Claremont, California

PAGEANT PRESS, INC.
NEW YORK

CONTENTS

chapter

1

MONEY AND ITS LEGAL QUALITIES

MONEY IN LAW AND ECONOMICS

THE PLACE OF MONEY IN THE LAW—IN THE FRAMEWORK of statutes, proclamations, administrative regulations and court decisions—has received considerable attention in both legal and economic literature. Most students of economics are somewhat familiar with the ideas of John Law and his attempts to provide France with an indefinitely expandable supply of paper currency possessed of almost all the properties royal prerogatives could provide. The twentieth century has produced other estimates of the legal aspects and significance of money, ranging from Knapp's *State Theory of Money* in 1905 to more modern and more scientific works such as those of Nussbaum[1] and Mann[2]. There are also hundreds of articles in the various law journals and economic publications. Many of the studies of money and banking also have been concerned with money's legal aspects.

A student might reasonably suppose that such an extensive literature would have developed a common meaning for the word *money*. Normally the citizen in his day-to-day affairs is careless in his use of the word, but lawyers and economists, who are under more rigid scientific compulsions, might be expected to be more precise. Unfortunately, this is not the case. Legal definitions as well as economic definitions vary widely. To complicate the literature still further, there has been considerable change in the most frequent usages over time. The simple fact is that there are no fixed or generally accepted definitions of the terms *money, credit* and *currency*.[3] Each writer in the field of money, therefore, is duty bound to explain his use of the words.

A convenient and appropriate usage for this monograph is to employ the term *money* to mean any generally accepted means of payment which circulates freely without reference to the credit standing of the person who passes it. Within this term it is possible to distinguish coined money, paper money and bank notes. Credit, then, can be used to mean checks, for example, which are subject to questions of the credit standing of the person signing the order. This usage corresponds closely enough to general understanding to avoid most of the problems of definition, although a good case can be made for confining *money* (which derives from the Latin *moneta* or mint) to minted coin, while substituting the word *currency* to include coin, paper money and bank notes.

Although the extent to which inconsistent vocabularies may be responsible is obscure, it will be quite apparent to anyone who makes even a cursory examination of court decisions and the pertinent literature over the last century that monetary economists, lawyers and legislators have often been unable to understand one another. This may be due, in part, to inertia or accident, to the fact that confusion and misunderstanding may sometimes be politically advantageous, or even to the development of a highly specialized educational process. Whatever the causes, the lawyer or legislator too often appears ignorant of the economic principles applicable to money and to monetary history. Not too infrequently the monetary economist or historian seems to be equally unaware of the legal questions involved in his field of specialization. Since each is concerned with different aspects of the same basic problem, the search for truth and for solutions to current problems calls logically for greater efforts to bridge the gap between legal and economic aspects of money and monetary issues.

LEGAL QUALITIES OF MONEY

If the reader is fortunate enough to have one of each of the three most important forms of paper money presently in use in the United States, he may note that the legal qualities of the bills—as stated on the faces—vary considerably. The United States note bears this inscription on the left side: "This note is a legal tender at its face value for all debts public and private." The silver certificate bears this inscription: "This certificate is legal tender for all debts, public and private." The third type of paper money, Federal Reserve notes, carry a very different inscription. It reads, "This note is legal tender for all debts, public and private, and is redeemable in lawful money at the United States Treasury, or at any Federal Reserve bank." As will be shown later, this quality of Federal Reserve notes dates from May 12, 1933; prior to that time these notes were "receivable by all national banks and member banks and Federal Reserve banks and for all taxes, customs, and other public dues," in accordance with the terms of the original Federal Reserve Act of December, 1913.

A brief survey of current money and banking textbooks, legal texts and legal and monetary treatises will convince the reader that there is a current lack of understanding of these qualities of money. No attempt has been made to catalogue the various inconsistencies and misunderstandings. Whenever such citations occur, the purpose is to bring order out of chaos, not to criticize any individual.

THREE QUALITIES OF MONEY IN AMERICAN LAW

The history of American monetary legislation clearly indicates that our lawmakers developed three distinct concepts of the qualities of money: legal tender, lawful money, and money made receivable for specified purposes. Although there are some elements of chance and local usage in the development of the qualities, they appear in laws passed in order to aid in the settlement of legal questions, to facilitate the administration and control of the monetary and banking structure, and to pervert money for an ulterior political purpose.

Historically, the quality of full legal tender has indicated the widest recognition which can be bestowed upon money by law or legal procedure. Generally speaking, there has been no superior quality of money in law although money not made legal tender could, of course, possess superior economic quality. Usually, but not always, the standard money has been legal tender; this quality, in other words, is most frequently a basic legal complement of the standard monetary unit. Laws dealing with the monetary standard, as the definition of a monetary unit in terms of a metal such as gold, often carry provisions describing the legal tender quality of the coins.

Although money other than the standard has been given the quality of legal tender, the more frequently observed practice in American law has been to make such other money receivable for certain specified purposes or in specified payments, such as taxes or other payments to a political authority, or to an instrumentality of that authority.

A third quality, that of lawful money, has been used to describe the kinds of money which could be used legally as reserves against bank notes or bank deposits, or which could be used as redemption funds held by an administrative authority such as the United States Treasury. This use of the term "lawful money" appears to be uniquely American.

NEED FOR SYSTEMATIC EXPOSITION OF PRINCIPLES

Unfortunately, the principles and interrelationships underlying these three legal qualities of money have never had a systematic and careful exposition, at least as far as the author has been able to determine. Often legislative authorities appear to have been ignorant of the principles involved, or even heedless or careless. The legal tender quality in particular has been used for such purposes as favoring debtors over creditors, or favoring government at the expense of all the people. It is easy to find polemics on the legal tender quality in the last half of the nineteenth century resulting from the "Greenback" experience of the Civil War. Here and there, too, one discovers odd versions of fiat theories of money which make money and legal tender identical.[4] But serious monetary treatises tend to avoid a discussion of the economic and political aspects of these qualities of money and, moreover, legal treatises have sometimes avoided the issues or have shown inconsistencies with respect to the legal aspects alone.

Monetary, legal and economic literature over the past half century reveals an almost negligible amount of discussion concerning legal qualities of money and, unfortunately, a good part of what does exist is erroneous. The most notable exception is the work of Professor Walter E. Spahr, Chairman of the Department of Economics at New York University's School of Commerce and Executive Vice-President of the Economists' National Committee on Monetary Policy, who has recognized the need for further clarification and analysis of our laws concerning these qualities of money.[5] Two excellent articles also appeared in the *Journal of Political Economy* in 1938; they recognized some of the inconsistencies and problems involved in the use of the term "lawful money" but did not relate it to the other concepts.[6] A volume entitled *What Are We Using for Money?* by Paul Bakewell, Jr.[7] contains a chapter entitled "Dollars and Lawful Money" and another entitled "Legal Tender." The basic purpose of the book, however, is not to formulate a fundamental understanding of the principles and, in the opinion of the author, is in error with respect to a number of assertions concerning the legal qualities of money.

With these few exceptions, it is necessary to reach back fifty years or more to Alva R. Hunt's *A Treatise on the Law of Tender, and Bringing Money into Court*[8] and to Sophonisba P. Breckinridge's *Legal Tender: A Study in British and American History*[9] in order to find a study of serious or scientific import relating to these matters. Both these studies, which appeared in 1903, were concerned almost entirely with the concept of legal tender. Hunt is concerned almost entirely with the lawyer's point of view; Miss Breckinridge is concerned exclusively with the historical point of view. It is probable, furthermore, that Miss Breckinridge's study appeared at a most inopportune time owing to the fact that greater consistency in the relations of the concepts occurred prior to 1900 than after. The remainder of the literature dealing with these concepts of the legal qualities of money is fugitive in nature, and widely dispersed.

Although probably the result of the fugitive nature of the material, there is, the student soon discovers, a widespread lack of scientific definition or classification of the qualities of legal tender, lawful money and money receivable for specified purposes. One finds money which is receivable in payments to governments called legal tender, legal tender erroneously called lawful money, and lawful money erroneously called legal tender.

This confusion of meaning is not confined to the lay public. It is found in many—in my opinion, most—economic treatises, in many court decisions, in laws passed by Congress, in laws passed by state legislatures and in opinions expressed by administrative authority.

For example, a recent treatise in the general field of monetary and fiscal policy stated:

> "National bank notes solved the problem of safety for the note-holder. People no longer had to worry about the soundness of the banks whose notes they held. One bank was as good as another—or as good as a United States Note ("greenback") issued by the Treasury. A businessman who held enough bank notes to pay off his debts as they matured could no longer be forced into bankruptcy—as many had been in the panics of 1837 and 1857—for lack of 'legal tender'. Under the National Banking System, bank notes were legal tender; and from 1879 onward they were also convertible into gold. . . ."[10]

Disregarding some of the other legal and economic implications of this paragraph, the fact of the matter is that national bank notes were not legal tender at any time during the period they were of significance in our monetary structure. They were never legal tender in the United States until May 12, 1933. During the period under discussion above, a private creditor could have refused to accept national bank notes at any time, solely on the grounds that the notes were not legal tender.[11] Some private creditors did so.

The purpose of the above citation is not to criticize the author whose contributions to the literature are well known. Many other similar unintentional errors could have been cited. Nor does it appear worthwhile to attempt to catalogue the multitude of misunderstandings which appear in economic literature. Some of the confusion which exists in statute law, in court decisions, and in administrative interpretations is treated more fully in Chapter VII.

LEGAL QUALITIES OF MONEY IN PRESENT LAWS

The monetary upheavals during the years 1933 and 1934 involved the abandonment of the gold coin standard in the United States and the substitution of what has been called "an international gold bullion standard,"[12] or a "limited" or "qualified" gold bullion standard[13] or an "administratively discretionary gold bullion standard."[14] The system resulting from the legislation adopted in 1933 to 1934 provided for only an indirect conversion of non-gold currency into the standard monetary unit. Domestically, if not internationally, it can be described accurately as an irredeemable paper money system. For all practical purposes within the economy, the Thomas Amendment to the Agricultural Adjustment Act of May 12, 1933, as amended by the Public Resolution of June 5, 1933, made all our coins and currency full legal tender. This legislation had the following unfortunate results (among others):

(1) One monetary law denied what another asserted.

(2) Administrative officials were forced to deny the validity of court decisions in order to avoid obvious accounting inconsistencies.

(3) The American economy was exposed to practices which, if employed, would be undesirable even though they might be within the letter of the law.

In later years, as will be demonstrated further, certain of these inconsistencies became so apparent that Congress was forced to act. The action taken by the Act of June 12, 1945, which reduced the reserve requirements from 40% in gold certificates against Federal Reserve notes outstanding to 25% and from 35% in lawful money to 25% in gold certificates against deposits in Federal Reserve banks, also outlawed all Treasury currency except gold certificates for use as a reserve against deposits. Instead of remedying the illogical situation which had existed, instead of facing the issues squarely, this act provided further illogical and inconsistent regulations. The legislators apparently did not understand the concepts concerning which they were attempting to legislate.

SIGNIFICANCE OF THE LEGAL QUALITIES OF MONEY

Whatever misunderstanding and confusion have prevailed, there is no warrant for supposing that the distinctions between these three legal qualities of money are unimportant, or that they may be disregarded as merely different aspects of the same thing. These qualities are distinct; they involve questions of justice, of sound accounting procedure, and of adequate and proper supervision and administration of monetary and banking systems.

The question of justice is a basic element in the concept of legal tender and has a direct bearing on the law of contract. Used in its technical sense, the concept of lawful money rests upon sound accounting procedure. So, too, does the concept of money made receivable for specified purposes. All three qualities or concepts involve principles of proper administration of a nation's monetary and banking structure.

All three qualities have long and involved histories, characterized by a variety of inconsistencies. Yet, out of the maze of conflicting detail, there emerge principles which provide rules for practical application. Since these three qualities and the principles underlying them involve fundamental differences, it is necessary that they be kept in separate categories in order to profit from the experiences of the past and thus obtain the benefits which may be secured from proper application of principle.

PURPOSE OF THIS STUDY

Present-day confusion of the legal qualities of legal tender, lawful money, and money receivable for specified purposes has resulted from ambiguous usage of the terms which, in turn, appears to rest upon failure to recognize the meanings, the significance, the interrelations, and the practical applications of the concepts.

All our money became full legal tender in 1933. This means only that all our money is equally good, in statute law, so far as making payments is concerned. It can also be said, with accuracy, that all our money is equally bad. It is not true, and it is difficult to see why anyone should have thought that it could be true, that all our money is equally good, or usable, so far as service as reserves against note issue and deposits is concerned.

What we have in practice, of course, is a system based upon promises to pay dollars with virtually no mechanism for insuring the continuity or stability of the basic monetary unit. Although we have most of the attributes that can be considered the essence of an inconvertible and irredeemable paper money standard, we still retain the semi-fiction that paper money is a promise to pay at some indefinite time, or if one prefers, on demand. The latter is technically correct. In fact, however, failure to pay or the impossibility of paying makes the former more accurate. Had the purposes of the legal qualities of money not been disregarded, we would have at least been faced with the necessity of saying of a piece of paper: "This IS a dollar."

Confusion of the legal qualities of money, and their significance, can only be remedied by examining the development of the concepts and the principles underlying them and then adopting the changes in our monetary laws which would eliminate the inconsistencies presently existing in them.

The present need is to provide a practical guide for students, bankers, legislators, lawyers, judges, administrators, economists and, to some extent, the general public. If the principles contained herein are applied to existing statutes, much of the confusion will disappear. To formulate specific recommendations requires a critical examination: (1) of the meaning of these three qualities of money, and of the concepts underlying them; (2) of the interrelationships of the concepts, and of the principles governing their application; (3) of the authority to specify how these qualities may be applied, and of the evolution of that authority; and (4) of the inconsistencies that have occurred in the historical development and application of these qualities. The purpose of this volume is to provide such a critical examination.

FOOTNOTES

1 Arthur Nussbaum, *Money in the Law* (Foundation Press, Inc., Chicago, 1939).

2 F. A. Mann, *The Legal Aspect of Money, with special reference to comparative, private and public international law* (Oxford University Press, London, 1953). This is a second edition of a work which first appeared in 1938.

3 See, for example, the brief but excellent statement on this subject in H. L. Reed, *Money, Currency and Banking* (McGraw-Hill Company, Inc., New York, 1942), pp. 1-2.

4 For example, Henri Cernuschi, *Nomisma; or "legal tender"* (D. Appleton and Company, New York, 1877). The book is composed of evidence and statements to the United States Monetary Commission in 1877. On page 7 there occurs the curious statement, ". . . Money is a value created by law to be a scale of valuation and a valid tender for payments. . . . If you suppose that gold is not money, is not legal tender—if you suppose that silver is not money, is not legal tender—the value of gold and the value of silver is lost." Most authorities on money and banking would disagree with statements of this kind which, incidentally, are presented with no evidence in support. It is surprising to note how frequently they appear.

5 For example, in his "Problems Caused by the Misconceptions of the Meaning of Legal Tender, Lawful Money, and Money Receivable for Specified Purposes," *Money and the Law* (New York University School of Law, New York, 1945), pp. 33-41; *It's Your Money* (Economists' National Committee on Monetary Policy, New York, 1946), pp. 9-24; and in his chapters on money and banking in Spahr and others, *Economic Principles and Problems* (Farrar and Rinehart, Inc., New York, 1940), 4th ed., Vol. I, pp. 434, 544-547. Dr. Spahr's observations concerning these concepts also have appeared in *Monetary Notes,* published monthly by the Economists' National Committee on Monetary Policy, and in numerous articles in *The Commercial and Financial Chronicle.*

6 Edward C. Simmons, "The Concept of Lawful Money," *Journal of Political Economy* (1938), Vol. XLVI, pp. 108-118; Ira B. Cross, "A Note on Lawful Money," *Journal of Political Economy* (1938), Vol. XLVI, pp. 409-413.

7 D. Van Nostrand Company, Inc., New York, 1952.

8 Frank P. Dufresne, St. Paul, Minn., 1903.

9 University of Chicago Press, Chicago, 1903.

10 Albert Gailord Hart, *Money, Debt and Economic Activity* (Prentice-Hall, Inc., New York, 1948), p. 28.

11 National bank notes were receivable for certain specified purposes and not for others. They were redeemable in lawful money which, until 1879, meant United States notes. The qualities of national bank notes are discussed in detail on pages 85-86.

12 Spahr and others, *op. cit.*, p. 444.

13 F. A. Bradford, *Money and Banking* (Longmans, Green and Co., New York, 1937), p. 90.

14 Roy W. McDonald, "Legal Aspects of Monetary Questions of Greatest Significance to the United States," *Money and the Law, op. cit.*, p. 65. See also Nussbaum, *op. cit.*, p. 189. The fact that there is considerable disagreement concerning the appropriate name for this condition illustrates the confusion which has resulted.

THE AUTHORITY TO DESIGNATE LEGAL QUALITIES OF MONEY

A

PRIOR TO THE ADOPTION OF THE CONSTITUTION OF THE UNITED STATES

THIS STUDY OF THE ORIGIN AND DEVELOPMENT OF THE authority to designate the legal qualities of money may be divided conveniently into two periods: (1) prior to the adoption of the Constitution of the United States and (2) from 1789 to the present time.

There are several reasons for this division. The use of all three concepts at the same time appears to be uniquely American; the legal meaning and wording in our law differ from those found in other law, including that of England. English law and English customs with respect to money were of much greater influence upon the legal qualities of our money before the adoption of the American Constitution than after. Furthermore, the separation of the qualities dates from approximately the beginning of the nineteenth century, although some distinction is apparent before that time. Last, and perhaps most important, is the fact that a study of the authority to designate the legal qualities of money is in large part a study of American constitutional law.

ANCIENT AND MEDIEVAL PERIODS

In the ancient world there may have been some recognition of one or more of the different qualities of money. The evidence, unfortunately, is immersed in a mass of detail. Professor Burns states that, although the evidence is based to some extent on inference, "it is beyond doubt that legal tender regulations existed in some form or other from the earliest times."[1] For the purposes of this study the evidence is insufficient to enable one to draw many significant conclusions.[2]

During the Middle Ages, and thereafter until 1700, there seems to have been no separation of various qualities of money. Kings considered the issuance of money a divine right and a primary source of income. Norman lords, for example, assumed the right to call in all money every three years, or in lieu thereof, to be paid a tax called a *monetagium.*[3] *Seignorage,* the difference between the bullion content of a coin and its face value, was also an important source of revenue.[4] Subsequent use of the legal tender quality to increase the revenues of the State reminds one of these early practices.

Prior to 1600, although rulers enforced the acceptance of moneys which they had coined, the words "legal tender" do not appear to have been employed. In so far as the authority to designate legal tender, or any other legal quality of money, is concerned, it was implicit in the power to coin money.

AUTHORITY IN ENGLAND PRIOR TO 1700

In England prior to 1700, the king possessed three powers with respect to money: (1) the power to coin money; (2) the power to charge a *seignorage* for that service; and (3) the power to determine the relative rates at which various coins, both domestic and foreign, should be valued in domestic payments.[5]

A royal proclamation or mint indenture declaring a coin "lawful money" or "current money" meant that it could be used without prejudice in all payments throughout the realm. Hence, all coins issued from the royal mint, or declared to be "current money" or "lawful money" by a royal proclamation, were legal tender in the modern sense of the word.[6] The words "legal tender" were not used at this time. "Tender" seems to have been used first to describe a defense to an action of debt, and was gradually absorbed into statutes to mean the money which could be used in paying a debt, as well as the legal defense itself.

A legal case, decided in 1601, clearly states the authority, as it then existed: "Where the condition was that Wade should pay £250 *legalis monet'Angliae,* it was resolved that Spanish silver so tendered was lawful money of England, for it was made current by proclamation in the time of the reign of Philip and Mary; also that French coins were current and lawful money of England by proclamation; and the King by his absolute prerogative may make foreign coin lawful money of England at his pleasure, by his proclamation."[7]

A transfer of authority from the king to parliament had occurred by about 1695.[8] For a period of years, however, both parliament and the Crown seem to have wielded the authority concurrently. In *Dixson v. Willoughs* the question arose as to whether gold guineas, coined at the royal mint, but without having received further legal recognition by act of parliament, could be considered capable of settling a debt; that is, legal tender. The court said: "Though there is no act of parliament or order of state for these guineas, yet being coined at the mint, and having the King's insignia upon them, they are lawful money at the value they were entered at the mint."[9]

There appears to have been no differentiation of legal qualities of money. All money duly recognized or authenticated was "lawful money" and legal tender.[10]

AUTHORITY IN ENGLAND AFTER 1700

After 1700, the authority to designate money "current money" or "lawful money" rested with the parliament. At first, all money recognized by parliament as current money was legal tender in the sense of being capable of use in any payment. By 1751, however, a specific designation of legal tender in statutes appears, as well as a limited recognition of other money which was not legal tender but similar to the concept of money receivable for specified purposes.[11] After 1797 only money specifically so designated was legal tender.[12] By the year 1797, and perhaps before that time, two distinct legal qualities of money had been recognized: legal tender, and money which, although not legal tender, could be paid and received in certain payments to the Crown, and could be paid and received between private persons where no objection was made to it.

The authority of parliament in recognizing more than one

quality of money and the practice of specifically designating legal tender is illustrated by the English Bank Act of 1797. During the war with Napoleon, notes of the Bank of England had become the chief means of payment. When a French man o' war appeared off the English coast the drain on the gold and silver reserves of the Bank of England was so great that it was forced to abandon redemption of its notes in coin on demand. The Bank Act, passed soon thereafter by parliament, did not make the notes of the bank legal tender, but accepted them in payments to the government and declared an offer of them to be "the equivalent of cash if made and accepted as such.[13]

The case of *Grigby v. Oakes et al.* tested the validity of the Bank Act, and adjudicated the question of the quality of the bank notes.[14]

Oakes and others were country bankers who had issued circulating notes, payable to the bearer on demand. Grigby demanded payment, refused to accept a Bank of England note, and insisted on payment in coin. The defendants argued that the language of the Bank Act, in making the notes the equivalent of cash, also made them legal tender. In rendering the decision, Chief Justice Lord Alvanley said: "If it had been intended by the legislature to make them [Bank of England notes] a good legal tender, that situation would have been expressed in such clear terms that no question could have arisen on the subject. . . . With respect to individuals it was not intended to prevent any creditor from captiously demanding payment in money, though such a creditor is deprived of the benefit of arresting his debtor. . . . Parliament and not this court must be applied to for a remedy." The Bank Act had specified payments to the Crown in which the Bank of England notes would be accepted. Judge Heath, in a concurring decision, used this as the basis for his reasoning. He said: ". . . The several provisions of the act making them [Bank of England notes] a good legal tender in certain excepted cases excludes the idea of their being so generally. . . ."

This decision clearly illustrated, in so far as Great Britain was concerned, that the authority to designate legal tender or other qualities of money was vested in parliament; that the quality of legal tender (in 1797) had to be granted specifically; and that describing bank notes as "the equivalent of cash, if made and accepted as such" is similar to the concept of money receivable for specified purposes, although those words were not used.

AUTHORITY IN THE AMERICAN COLONIES

Parliament considered that the authority which it possessed in England extended to the American Colonies. Colonial legislatures, however, designated money legal tender and receivable for specified purposes, whether or not they had the legal power to do so.

In 1749 several Colonies sent representatives to parliament to argue that the power to designate money legal tender had been granted to the Colonies by the Crown as a part of their charter privileges.[15] Their argument failed to convince parliament.

In 1751 parliament passed an act entitled "An act to regulate and restrain paper bills of credit in His Majesty's Colonies or Plantations of Rhode Island and Providence, Connecticut, the Massachusetts Bay, and New Hampshire, in America, and to prevent the same being legal tender in Payments for Money."[16]

This act instructed the Colonies' governors to veto acts of the legislatures or assemblies authorizing the emission of bills of credit except under specified conditions. The excepted conditions included receiving them in payments to the Colonial Treasuries and retiring them, and special emergencies, such as war, when the consent of the home government would be granted. In 1763 the act was extended to include all British Colonies in North America, and amended to prohibit all bills of credit, whether legal tender or merely receivable by the Colonial Treasuries.[17] In 1773 the conditions were modified once more to permit bills which were not legal tender but "receivable by the public treasurers in the Colonies in the payment of any duties, taxes, or other debts due to the said public treasurers."[18]

All the Colonial legislatures, at one time or another between

1690 and 1762, made paper money legal tender. Apparently the authority was exercised illegally. The legislatures also made paper money receivable for taxes and other payments to the Colonial treasurers; sometimes with authority granted to them by parliament, sometimes without such authority.[19]

AUTHORITY UNDER THE ARTICLES OF CONFEDERATION

Under the Articles of Confederation, the Continental Congress was not specifically granted the authority to designate money legal tender or to give money any other legal quality. The question of whether it was without the authority to designate money receivable in payments to the Continental Treasurer is a moot question. It seems doubtful, however, for the Continental Congress had no power to tax. On the other hand, if it could organize or authorize a bank, such as the Bank of North America, it seems reasonable to suppose that it could have stated what money would be receivable by the bank, and that the money issued by the bank would be received by the Continental Treasurer. In general, the powers not specifically granted to the Congress were retained by the individual states.

The following sections of the Articles of Confederation delineate the extent of the authority of the Continental Congress in matters concerning money:

"Article II. Each state retains its sovereignty, freedom and independence, and every power, jurisdiction and right, which is not by this confederation expressly delegated to the united states in congress assembled . . .

"Article IX . . . The united states in congress assembled shall also have the sole and exclusive right and power of regulating the alloy and value of coin struck by their own authority, or by that of the respective states—fixing the standard of weights and measures throughout the united states . . .

"The united states in congress assembled shall never . . . coin money, nor regulate the value thereof . . . nor emit bills, nor borrow money on the credit of the united states, nor appropriate money . . . unless nine states assent to the same . . ."[20]

The Continental Congress never attempted to confer, by its own action, the quality of legal tender upon any coin or paper money. It passed a law providing for the establishment of a mint, and authorized coinage of a silver dollar containing 375-64/100 grains of fine silver, and a gold dollar containing 24-62/100 grains of fine gold, but said nothing about the legal qualities of the coins to be minted.[21] The coins were never minted, and one can only assume that the designation would have been made, if at all, by the several states.

In 1775, after issuing paper money promises to pay these dollars, Congress recommended to "the legislatures of the united states to pass laws to make the bills of Congress, issued by the Congress, a lawful tender in the payment of public and private debts, and a refusal thereof an extinguishment of such debts."[22]

Legislatures of the thirteen states designated the Continental Currency, as well as their own paper money, legal tender without limitation. Some of the states declared the Continental Currency legal tender before Congress recommended that they do so; others afterward. Some included the paper money of other states as legal tender in addition to their own.

Under the Articles of Confederation, therefore, the authority to designate the legal qualities of money was vested exclusively in the several states. The facts are: (1) Congress was not given the authority specifically; (2) all powers not *expressly* granted were reserved to the states; and (3) Congress never attempted to exercise such an authority.

B

AUTHORITY UNDER THE CONSTITUTION OF THE UNITED STATES

PERTINENT SECTIONS OF THE CONSTITUTION

The sections of the Constitution of the United States relevant to a discussion of the authority to designate the various qualities of money are:

Article I, Section 8. "The Congress shall have Power to lay and collect Taxes, Duties, Imposts and Excises . . .; To borrow Money, . . . to coin Money, regulate the Value thereof, and of Foreign Coin, and fix the Standard of Weights and Measures; . . . To make all Laws which shall be necessary and proper for carrying into Execution the foregoing Powers, and all other Powers vested by this Constitution in the Government of the United States, or in any Department or Officer thereof."

Article I, Section 9. "No . . . ex post facto Law shall be passed."

Article I, Section 10. "No State shall . . . coin Money; emit Bills of Credit; make any Thing but gold and silver Coin a Tender in Payment of Debts; pass any . . . ex post facto Law, or Law impairing the Obligation of Contracts . . ."

Amendment V. "No person . . . shall be deprived of life, liberty, or property, without due process of law; nor shall private property be taken for public use, without just compensation."

Amendment X. "The powers not delegated to the United States by the Constitution, nor prohibited by it to the States, are reserved to the States respectively or to the people."[23]

The nature of the authority granted to the Congress and to the states, with respect to money, is not explicit. The Constitution did not specifically forbid the issuance of paper money by Congress; it did not forbid Congress to make anything legal tender, nor did it specifically grant it the power to do so; it did not forbid the issuance of paper money by individuals, associations or corporations, nor did it forbid either Congress or the states to receive such money or to regulate its issuance. The interpretation of the extent of authority to designate legal tender, lawful money and money receivable for specified purposes thus becomes a matter of judicial decision.

AUTHORITY OF THE STATES TO DESIGNATE LEGAL TENDER

At the present time, as a result of Federal court decisions

and acquiescence by the states in Congress' use of the authority, legal tender is designated exclusively by Congress.

This seems to be somewhat at variance with the letter and spirit of the Constitution. By forbidding the states to make anything except gold and silver coins legal tender, or to pass a law impairing the obligation of contracts, the intent of the framers of the Constitution seems plain. The states were to have the power to designate legal tender, as they had under the Articles of Confederation, but the money upon which the quality could be conferred was limited to gold and silver coin. Any other interpretation makes the restriction upon the states meaningless and redundant. If state courts were to adhere strictly to the letter and spirit of the Constitution, they would never render a decision saying that anything except gold or silver coin is a legal tender.[24]

The transfer of authority from the states to Congress seems to have occurred for three reasons: (1) the first coinage act of April 2, 1792, made the gold and silver coins authorized legal tender, and apparently no one questioned the authority of Congress to do so; (2) Federal courts have not questioned the apparent contention of Congress that the power to coin money included the power to designate legal tender;[25] and (3) the belief that the power to determine the standard money necessitated making that money legal tender may have influenced the transfer of authority.

AUTHORITY OF CONGRESS TO DESIGNATE LEGAL TENDER

By virtue of the decisions rendered by the Supreme Court of the United States, Congress has the authority to confer the quality of legal tender upon any money, to the exclusion of the restricted power of the states, provided Congress exercises that power.[26] There are some unsettled questions, however. One is the question of whether the authority may be delegated implicitly to an administrative agent, such as a military commander of an occupied territory.[27] Another question is what remedy, if any, is available, if damages can be proved as a result of an illegal exercise of Congress' authority (that is, one which violated a restriction on the authority, such as the power of the United States to abrogate certain of its contracts with private individuals).[28]

Two sets of legal cases have established the limits of the power of Congress with respect to legal tender. The first set is concerned with the legal tender quality of United States notes, which were first issued February 25, 1862.[29] The second set is concerned with Congress' action in prohibiting the circulation of legal tender gold coin and gold certificates and in making all money legal tender by the Act of May 12, 1933, and the Joint Resolution of June 5, 1933.[30]

The legal tender decisions concerning the issuance of United States notes answered some, but not all, of the questions relating to the authority of Congress to designate money legal tender. In *Hepburn v. Griswold,* the Court decided that the power to make United States notes a legal tender for private contracts was beyond the constitutional authority of Congress when the contracts were entered into prior to the passage of the act. No question of authority in the case of contracts entered into after the passage of the act was involved in this decision. The Court specifically pointed out that there might be a different decision if contracts were entered into after passage of the act. The majority of the Court, in a 5-3 decision, reasoned as follows: (1) the power to make these notes legal tender was not specifically granted to Congress; (2) the power was not implied, nor incident to other powers granted, such as the power to coin money, to borrow money or to wage war; (3) the power impaired the obligation of contracts and violated the spirit of the fifth amendment.

The cases of *Knox v. Lee* and *Parker v. Davis* involved a reconsideration of the *Hepburn v. Griswold* decision by a reconstituted Supreme Court. This decision denied that there was a distinction between contracts entered into before and after the legal tender act of 1862, and argued the question anew. The power of Congress to issue legal tender notes was declared to be a power incident to the powers to borrow money and wage war, and, therefore, a legitimate exercise of congressional authority in time of war. Whether it was also a legitimate exercise of congressional authority in time of peace as well was left unanswered.

A new issue of legal tender notes in 1878[31] raised the question of whether or not Congress could make such notes a legal tender in time of peace. In *Juilliard v. Greenman,* the Court decided that the power to make the notes legal tender was a legitimate exercise of congressional authority at any time. The Court argued that the power to coin money was a universally recognized power of sovereign governments. The Court said: "The power is incident to the power of borrowing money and issuing bills or notes of the government for money borrowed, of impressing upon these notes the quality of being a legal tender for the payment of private debts, was a power universally understood to belong to sovereignty in Europe and America at the time of framing the Constitution of the United States."

In summary, the reasoning of the majority decision was that the designation of the notes as legal tender was incident to the power to coin money and regulate the value thereof; that it was incident to the power to borrow money; and that it was a power commonly accepted as belonging to sovereign governments.[32]

There were several questions which these decisions did not examine. They did not establish (1) whether Congress could make a specific exception as to the acceptance of legal tender money in certain payments to the United States; (2) whether it could compel the individual states to accept them in payment of taxes and other debts to the state governments; and (3) whether its power extended to contracts specifying coin of a given weight and fineness or to contracts specifying gold or silver bullion.

In *Cheang-Kee v. United States*[33] the Court held that it was within the power of Congress to refuse to accept legal tender United States notes in particular kinds of payments to the United States, such as duties on imports.[34]

The decisions are not clear with respect to the question of whether or not individual states may refuse to accept money made legal tender by an act of Congress. A state court decided that a judgment for taxes payable to a state was a debt within the meaning of the legal tender acts, and could be discharged by legal tender United States notes.[35] In *Lane County v. Oregon,* on the other hand, the Supreme Court decided that Congress, by the legal tender acts, has not intended to force a state to accept United States notes in payment of taxes.[36] The Court did not decide whether or not Congress could have done so had it so intended.

Prior to 1933, Congress' authority to designate legal tender commonly was thought to be limited by the Supreme Court decision in the case of *Bronson v. Rodes.*[37] The question in that case was whether or not contracts expressed in terms of coin or bullion could be discharged, dollar for dollar, by any legal tender. Chief Justice Chase, in *Bronson v. Rodes,* decided that a contract stipulating payment in gold coin was not a "debt" within the meaning of the legal tender act.[38] His judgment required payment in gold coin. This decision did not resolve the question of authority, however, inasmuch as it merely stated that Congress had not intended to include these contracts within the group which could be discharged by paying United States notes. In *Trebilcock v. Wilson*[39] the *Bronson* decision was reaffirmed by the same Court which had overruled the *Hepburn v. Griswold* decision.

Neither the *Bronson* case nor the *Trebilcock* case specifically stated that Congress' authority was limited to contracts expressed in terms of dollars in general. Both decisions were rendered in such a way as to interpret the *intent* of Congress in the legal tender acts. Both decisions referred to the fact that Congress had authoritzed two different kinds of money, and had itself exercised an option to require payment in one kind rather than another, although both were legal tender.

For example, in *Bronson v. Rodes,* the Court said: "It is a just if not a necessary inference from the fact that both descriptions of money were issued by the same government, that contracts to pay in either were equally sanctioned by law. . . ." Similarly, in *Trebilcock v. Wilson* the Court states: ". . . The terms, in specie, are merely descriptive of the kind of dollars in which the note is payable, there being different kinds in circulation, recognized by law."

Many decisions concerning specie contracts were rendered

during the period 1862 to 1880. The majority are in agreement that such contracts cannot be discharged by any legal tender, dollar for dollar. There is considerable variation, however, with respect to the judgment rendered. Some required payment in the particular money mentioned in the contract, such as gold coin. Others provided for payment in legal tender money, but in an amount equivalent to the value of the particular kind of money specified in the contract, such as payment of the value of a particular amount of gold in United States notes.[40]

Under these decisions, the favorable experience of creditors who had contracts calling for coin or bullion, in contrast with those whose contracts were expressed simply in dollars, caused widespread use of a gold clause in public and private contracts. The terminology of the gold clause varied, but the obvious intent in all cases was to adopt a commercial standard of deferred payments for the contract in the event that Congress should again alter its definition of standard money. The greenback experience engendered considerable mistrust in the wisdom and integrity of Congress in respect to monetary legislation. Private parties tried to choose that measure of value in deferred payments which, in their opinion, best served that function. Government obligations, too, often had a gold clause promising payment in gold coin equal to the standard of weight and fineness on the date of the loan.[41]

By Public Resolution of June 5, 1933, Congress resolved that "any obligation which purports to give the obligee a right to require payment in gold or a particular kind of coin or currency, or in an amount in money of the United States measured thereby, is declared to be against public policy. . . . Every obligation, heretofore or hereafter incurred . . . shall be discharged upon payment, dollar for dollar, in any coin or currency which at the time of payment is legal tender for public and private debts. . . ."[42] The Resolution then declared that all money of the United States was full legal tender.[43]

In the case of *Nortz v. United States*,[44] a former owner of gold certificates, payable on demand in gold coin of the former weight and fineness, brought suit to recover $1.69 in currency for every dollar of the gold certificates which he had surrendered to the Treasury. He contended that the gold certificates were promises to pay gold dollars weighing 25.8 grains, 9/10 fine (the previous legal definition of a dollar), although a subsequent presidential proclamation had redefined the dollar as 15 5/21 grains of gold, 9/10 fine.

The Court refused to accept the plaintiff's argument, and ruled that he was only entitled to recover what the gold coin would have been worth at the time he surrendered the certificates. Public Resolution No. 10 of June 5, 1933, said the Court, was within the constitutional authority of Congress because Congress had the power to protect the nation's physical resources and the power to coin money and to provide a medium of exchange.

In the case of *Norman v. Baltimore and Ohio Railroad*,[45] a suit was brought upon a bond coupon which promised payment of so many dollars "in gold coin of the United States of the present standard of weight and fineness."[46] The Court held that parties to a private contract could provide for payment only in the currency designated by law *at the time of payment*. Any other interpretation, in the opinion of the Court, would interfere with the power of Congress to provide a uniform currency. The Court said: "It requires no acute analysis or profound economic inquiry to disclose the dislocation of the domestic economy which would be caused by such a disparity of conditions in which, it is insisted, those debtors under gold clauses should be required to pay one dollar and sixty-nine cents in currency while respectively receiving their taxes, rates, charges and prices on the basis of one dollar of that currency."

In the author's opinion, the Court failed to face the real issues involved. Two questions should have been answered unequivocally: (1) Does the Congress have the power to define the monetary standard at its whim and pleasure? (2) Does the Congress have the power to designate anything at all a legal tender, irrespective of the definition of the monetary standard, and without regard to the nature or date of private contracts entered into in contemplation of law?

Apparently the decision answers both questions affirmatively, but the reasoning does not reveal an understanding of the questions on the part of the Court. The decision stated that, "Enforcement of the gold clause would produce, in other words, a dual monetary system." But no question concerning a dual or multiple currency system was involved; the question concerned the power of Congress to alter the monetary standard. This, and the other arguments of the Court, were beside the point. The second question was not answered directly by the Court.

The decision of the Court in the case of *Perry v. United States*[47] is the most paradoxical of the three decisions. Perry held a United States Liberty Loan Bond which bore an express promise to pay both principal and interest in "United States gold coin of the present standard of value."[48] He brought suit to recover damages sustained when payment was made in currency subsequently made legal tender at a new standard of value. He asked $1.69 in currency for every dollar of the former standard promised in the bond. He contended that it was beyond the power of Congress to violate the pledge made by the United States to redeem the bond in gold as pledged.

The Court decided that Public Resolution No. 10 of June 5, 1933, was unconstitutional as applied to gold clauses in government contracts with private individuals. But, in assessing damages, it concluded that no damages had been sustained and none could be collected. "We conclude," said the Chief Justice, "that the Joint Resolution of June 5, 1933, insofar as it attempted to override the obligation of the bond in suit, went beyond the Congressional power. . . .

"In considering what damages, if any, the plaintiff has sustained by the alleged breach of his bond, it is hence inadmissible to assume that he was entitled to obtain gold coin for recourse to foreign markets or for dealing in foreign exchange, or for other purposes contrary to the control over gold coin which the Congress had the power to exert, and had exerted in its monetary legislation. . . .

"Plaintiff demands the 'equivalent' in currency of the gold coin promised. But 'equivalent' cannot mean more than the amount of money which the promised gold coin would be worth to the bondholder for the purposes for which it could legally be used."

Much of the decision in this case, as in that of *Norman v. Baltimore and Ohio Railroad,* seems to be a waste of words. Again the question was not faced squarely, for the question here was simply: Does Congress have the power to abrogate its own contracts? The Court said it did, but in such a devious manner that it appeared to have denied it in words, while admitting it in deed. Furthermore, it is difficult, if not impossible, to reconcile this decision with that rendered in the case of *Nortz v. United States,* which also involved the abrogation of a contract evidenced by a gold certificate instead of a bond.

If these decisions stand without modification, it seems apparent that the Congress has the authority to alter the monetary standard at its pleasure, and to designate anything it pleases a legal tender in payment. In other words, Congress has the power to abrogate any or all contracts, public or private.

AUTHORITY OF THE STATES TO DESIGNATE LAWFUL MONEY

The several states have the power to designate or define lawful money, in the technical sense, as reserves of banks chartered under their laws, but this power is subject to the superior power of Congress. At the present time, for example, states may define lawful money for reserves of banks which are not members of the Federal Reserve System.

The authority to charter banks includes the power to regulate them, and the definition or designation of lawful money is a significant method of regulation. There can be no doubt that the states have the power to charter banks. In the case of *McCulloch v. Maryland*[49] the Supreme Court decided that Congress had the power to charter banks, but no one questioned the authority of the states to do so.

From 1838 to 1863, as far as this author has been able to determine, only the states exercised the authority to designate lawful money as a method of bank regulation. Thereafter the authority was exercised concurrently with the federal government.

AUTHORITY OF CONGRESS TO DESIGNATE
LAWFUL MONEY

Apparently the Congress of the United States has the supreme and exclusive authority to designate or define lawful money for any purpose, by virtue of the powers granted to it by the Constitution as interpreted by the federal courts. Up to the present time, however, Congress has not seen fit to exclude the states from a concurrent exercise of that authority.

The federal courts have not delineated clearly the extent of Congress' authority with respect to lawful money.[50] The Supreme Court has sustained acts of Congress which incorporated banks having the power to issue money,[51] established a national banking system and taxed state bank notes out of existence,[52] and created a Federal Reserve Banking System with supervision and regulation by a federal board.[53] By inference, Congress also possesses the authority to define or designate lawful money for reserve purposes or redemption purposes in state banks. It seems reasonable to assume that it also possesses the authority to exclude the states from exercising any authority at all over lawful money if it chooses. One authority on constitutional law states: "There would seem to be no constitutional objection to the monopolization of the banking field by the national government by bringing all commercial banking institutions into the Federal Reserve System. . . . The national authority over the subjects of revenue, finance, and currency is broad enough to embrace the important functions of every commercial bank."[54]

AUTHORITY TO DESIGNATE MONEY RECEIVABLE IN
PAYMENTS BY PRIVATE PERSONS TO GOVERNMENTS

The authority to designate money receivable by a government in payments to itself is based upon the power to tax and to borrow money. Both the states and the federal government have these powers. Both, therefore, have the power to designate money which they will receive for such purposes. The authority of the states is limited by the superior power of Congress with respect to all matters concerning money.

Congress made the notes of the First Bank of the United States receivable in payments to the United States. The authority for doing so is clearly expressed in a letter from Alexander Hamilton to President Washington in 1791:

"To designate or appoint the *money* or *thing* in which taxes are to be paid, is not only a proper but a *necessary exercise* of the power of collecting them. Accordingly Congress, in the law concerning the collection of the duties on imports and tonnage, have provided that they shall be paid in gold and silver. But while it was an indispensable part of the work to say in what they should be paid, the choice of the specific thing was mere matter of discretion. The payment might have been required in the commodities themselves. . . .

"No part of this can, it is presumed, be disputed. The appointment, then, of the *money* or *thing* in which taxes are to be paid, is an incident to the power of collection. And among the expedients which may be adopted, is that of bills issued under the authority of the United States."[55]

The Supreme Court upheld the validity of the act of Congress chartering the First Bank of the United States, notes of which were made receivable in payments to the United States, in the case of *McCulloch v. Maryland.*[56]

An act of Congress providing for the issuance of Treasury notes which "shall be everywhere received in payment of all duties and taxes levied by authority of the United States" was held to be constitutional in the case of *Thorndike v. United States.*[57] The Court argued that it was a necessary and proper exercise of the power to tax and the power to borrow money.

In the case of *Woodruff v. Trapnall,* the Supreme Court held that the State of Arkansas had the power to charter a bank, and to provide that the notes of the bank "shall be received in payment of all debts due to the State of Arkansas."[58]

State courts have repeatedly asserted that a state may provide by law for the payment of taxes, debts or other obligations due it in bank notes, scrip, land warrants or anything it sees fit to prescribe, by virtue of its power to tax.[59]

AUTHORITY TO DESIGNATE MONEY RECEIVABLE IN PAYMENTS BY GOVERNMENTS TO PRIVATE PERSONS

Neither the Supreme Court, other federal courts, nor the state courts seem to have defined clearly the extent of this authority or the basis of the authority. Authority to designate money receivable in payments by governments to private persons approaches authority to designate legal tender. A government having the authority to designate legal tender doubtless could use the more limited designation.

Both the state governments and Congress have exercised the authority, although less often than the authority to designate money receivable in payments to governments.

National bank notes, among other qualities,[60] were declared to be receivable "for all salaries and other debts and demands owing by the United States to individuals, corporations and associations within the United States, except interest on the public debt and in redemption of the national currency."[61] Apparently this type of receivability clause has not been used since that time in federal statute, although Section 18, paragraph 6, of the Federal Reserve Act provided for Federal Reserve bank notes to be issued under the same terms and conditions as national bank notes.[62]

Notes issued by the State of Missouri in 1828 were made receivable for all salaries and fees of office by civil and military employees of the state, and by certain state corporations. The Supreme Court decided that these notes were bills of credit within the meaning of the Constitution, and that the act of issuing them was unconstitutional. The Court said: "It seems impossible to doubt the intention of the legislature in passing this act, or to mistake the character of these certificates, or the office they were to perform. The denominations of the bills, from ten dollars to fifty cents, fitted them for the purposes of ordinary circulation; and their reception in payment of taxes and debts due to the government and to corporations, and of salaries and fees, would give them currency. They were to be put into circulation, that is, emitted by the government."[63] The qualities of the notes seem to have had some influence on the decision, but the fact that they were issued by and were direct obligations of the state also had a major influence.

In the case of *Briscoe et al. v. Bank of the Commonwealth of Kentucky,* however, the Supreme Court held that bank notes issued by a State-owned bank, and receivable in payments to the state and in payments to state creditors, could not be construed as bills of credit within the meaning of the Constitution.[64]

It appears, therefore, that states may designate money receivable in payments *by* the states *to* their creditors, subject to the limitations placed upon them by the Constitution of the United States.

AUTHORITY TO DESIGNATE MONEY RECEIVABLE IN PAYMENTS BY PRIVATE PERSONS TO CORPORATIONS OR ASSOCIATIONS

The authority to designate money receivable in payments by private persons to corporations or associations appears to be based upon (1) the legal principle of "set-off" or "offset," and (2) the authority to regulate banking institutions. The authority has been exercised both by the states and by Congress.

The common law, in general, allows a person who is both debtor and creditor to another person, to use the credit due him to cancel an equivalent amount of the indebtedness held against him. This principle has been applied often to notes or bills issued by banks. In addition to the common law principle, an equivalent right frequently was restated specifically in state laws with reference to banks. For example, the revised statutes of the State of Maine in 1857 stated: "Every bank shall receive its own bills, if offered in payment of its dues."[65]

State courts have consistently decided that banks chartered under the laws of the state shall receive their own bills or notes in payment of debts due them. The offer of such notes to an issuing bank by a debtor of the bank has the same effect as if legal tender money were offered.[66]

The power of states to designate such bills or notes receivable in such payments was sustained by the Supreme Court of the United States in the case of *United States v. Robertson*. Chief Justice Marshall, who delivered the decision stated: "On the ninth of February, 1819, the legislature of Maryland passed an act declaring that in payment of any debt due to, or judgment obtained by, any bank within that State, the note of such bank should be received. This act, so far as respects debts on which judgments have not been obtained, embodies the general and just principle respecting offsets which are of common application. Every debtor may pay his creditor with the notes of that creditor."[67]

Congress may have had this principle in mind when the National Bank Act, as amended, was passed in 1864. Section 32 of the act provided that: "Every association formed or existing under the provisions of this act shall take and receive at par for any liability to the said association any and all notes or bills issued by any association, existing under and by virtue of this act."

Whether or not the Congress had the principle of offset in mind, the device of making the bills receivable by the banks was a means of promoting the circulation of all national bank notes at par throughout the country. It was, therefore, an important instrument in the regulation of the currency.

Section 16 of the Federal Reserve Act of 1913 made the Federal Reserve notes "receivable by all national banks and member banks and Federal Reserve banks and for all taxes, customs and other public dues." The latter clause is the familiar and common quality of being receivable in payments to governments; the former clause extended the receivability provision of national bank notes to include all payments to these banks, rather than debts or liabilities alone. Only banks chartered under federal law were included, however, and the right of state banks to refuse the notes, if they wished, was retained until 1933.

Although the Supreme Court has never ruled specifically that Congress had the power to bestow this type of receivability on money, the extent of its authority to designate legal tender has been sustained. Because the former authority is much more limited in scope than the legal tender power, it seems obvious that it is within the power of Congress to do so.

FOOTNOTES

1 Arthur R. Burns, *Money and Monetary Policy in Early Times* (Alfred A. Knopf, New York, 1927), p. 378.
2 The three qualities of money under consideration in this study are relatively modern. To attempt to trace them in detail to ancient and medieval periods is of doubtful value if, in fact, the evidence is not completely obscured. Some of the studies investigating the early history of money in general are: W. W. Carlile, *The Evolution of Modern Money* (Macmillan and Co., Ltd., London, 1901); J. R. McCulloch, *Odd and Scarce Tracts on Money* (P. S. King and Son, Ltd., London, 1933); William Ridgeway, *The Origin of Metallic Currency and Weight Standards* (John Wilson and Son, Inc., Cambridge, Mass., 1892). Legal tender is referred to in these studies, but one can never be sure that the meaning is the same as that employed in this study.
3 W. J. Ashley, *An Introduction to English Economic History and Theory: The Middle Ages* (Longmans, Green and Co., New York, 1898), third ed., p. 168.
4 Edwin W. Kemmerer, *Gold and the Gold Standard* (McGraw-Hill Book Co., Inc., New York, 1944), p. 22.
5 Charles Jenkinson, 1st Earl of Liverpool, *A Treatise on the Coins of the Realm; in a letter to the King* (E. Wilson, London, 1880), p. 16.
6 That is, they could be used in any and all payments. Penalties for refusing them varied.
7 *Wade's Case,* 5 Coke 114 (1601).
8 Liverpool, *op. cit.,* pp. 79-80.
9 3 Salkeld 238 (1702).
10 S. P. Breckinridge, *Legal Tender* (University of Chicago Press, Chicago, 1903), p. 44.
11 24 Geo. II, c. 53 (1751). This act is discussed with reference to the American colonies on page 21.
12 Rogers Ruding, *Annals of the Coinage of Britain and Its Dependencies* (John Hearne, London, 1840), 3d ed., Vol. II, pp. 330-344.
13 37 Geo. III, c. 45 (1797).
14 2B. & P. 525 (1801).
15 *Journal of the House of Commons* (May-September, 1749), Vol. XXV, pp. 152, 814.
16 24 Geo. II, c. 503 (1751).

[17] 4 Geo. III, c. 35 (1763).

[18] 13 Geo. III, c. 57 (1773).

[19] There can be no doubt that the Colonial legislatures wanted the authority to designate money legal tender, or that they considered the action of parliament regulating their use of this authority unjust. This seems to have been a source of friction between the Colonies and the mother country that is commonly overlooked or minimized in studies of our economic history.

[20] James D. Richardson, *A Compilation of the Messages and Papers of the Presidents* (Bureau of National Literature, Inc., New York, 1897), Vol. I, pp. 5, 11.

[21] *Journals of Congress* (August 8, 1786), Vol. XI, p. 129.

[22] *Journals of Congress* (January 14, 1777), Vol. III, p. 19. This positive penalty for refusing legal tender differs from the present interpretation, and generally is an exception to the normal penalties. Other positive penalties enforced during this period are discussed on page 51.

[23] Richardson, *op. cit.,* pp. 18, 19, 20, 29-30.

[24] This appears to have been the reasoning in the court's decision in *Gwin v. Breedlove,* 2 How. 29 (1844).

[25] There is no evidence that the question of authority was raised by Congress in passing the first coinage act. *Journals of Congress* (December 26, 1791 to April 2, 1792), pp. 130-342.

[26] Congress has always exercised the power.

[27] This question is raised and discussed in Walter E. Spahr, *Allied Military Currency* (Economists' National Committee on Monetary Policy, New York, 1943), pp. 12, 18-21, and by Donald L. Kemmerer, "Allied Military Currency in Constitutional and International Law," *Money and the Law* (New York University School of Law, New York, 1945), pp. 89-91.

[28] This question was not decided in the case of *Perry v. United States,* 55 Sup. Ct. Rep. 457, 294 U. S. 330, because no damages were sustained by the plaintiff.

[29] The so-called "Legal Tender Cases": *Hepburn v. Griswold,* 8 Wall. 603 (1869); *Knox v. Lee, Parker v. Davis,* 12 Wall. 457 (1873); *Juilliard v. Greenman,* 110 U. S. 421 (1884).

[30] The so-called "Gold Clause Cases": *Norman v. Baltimore and Ohio Railroad Co.,* 294 U. S. 240 (1935); *Nortz v. United States,* 294 U. S. 317 (1935); *Perry v. United States,* 294 U. S. 330 (1935).

[31] Act of May 31, 1878, 20 *Statutes at Large* 87.

[32] Detailed analyses of the Court's reasoning, discussions of minority opinions and a description of the circumstances of the change in the Court after the first Legal Tender decision are available elsewhere; for example, in E. J. James, *The Legal Tender Decisions* (American Economic Association, Evanston, Ill., 1889); D. H. Chamberlain, "The 'Legal Tender' Decision of 1884," *American Law Review* (1884), Vol. XVIII, pp. 410-426; T. H. Talbot, "The 'Legal Tender' Decision

of 1884: Reply to Governor D. H. Chamberlain," *American Law Review* (1884), Vol. XVIII, pp. 618-634; Breckinridge, *op. cit.*, pp. 160-169.

[33] 70 U. S. 320 (1865).

[34] By the Act of March 10, 1866 (14 *Statutes at Large* 5), income tax returns were required to include a statement as to the nature of the income; that is, whether it was coin or United States notes. If the income consisted of coin, the assessor was required to increase the assessment to its equivalent value in United States notes. As far as the author has been able to determine, the validity of this section has never been ruled upon in the courts. The income tax assessment itself was subsequently declared unconstitutional.

[35] *Rhodes v. O'Farrell,* 2 Nev. 60 (1866).

[36] 74 U. S. 71 (1868).

[37] 74 U. S. 229 (1868).

[38] The unusual construction of the word "debts" in this case is discussed on page 105.

[39] 79 U. S. 687 (1871).

[40] For example, *Butler v. Horwitz,* 74 U. S. 258 (1869); *Thompson v. Butler,* 95 U. S. 694 (1877); *Gregory v. Morris,* 96 U. S. 619 (1878); *United States v. Erie Railway Co.,* 106 U. S. 327 (1882); *Brown v. Welch,* 26 Ind. 116 (1866); *Schoenberger v. Watts,* 10 Am. Law Reg. (pa.) 553 (1862); *Warinbold v. Schlicting,* 16 Iowa 243 (1864); *Whetstone v. Colley,* 36 Ill. 328 (1865); *Galliano v. Pierre,* 18 La. Ann. 10 (1866).

[41] Types of gold clauses are discussed by John T. Madden and Marcus Nadler in their *Gold Clause* (Institute of International Finance, New York, 1929), Bulletin No. 27. The authors estimate that more than $50 billion of publicly offered securities had some kind of gold clause.

[42] 48 *Statutes at Large* 112.

[43] When a currency is convertible into gold coin at par, and there is no fear of a suspension of this convertibility or of a devaluation, holders of gold coin contracts are willing to accept any form of paper currency, and even checks, without question. Because of the added convenience, they may prefer these means of payment. From the time of the resumption of specie payments in 1879 to March 3, 1933, contracts containing a gold clause gave nothing to the creditor which he would not have possessed otherwise, and constituted no additional burden upon the debtor in any way. The monetary legislation of 1933 and 1934 altered the meaning of the parties to contracts entered into before that time, but in contemplation of the law as it then existed. It impaired the obligation of contracts in any reasonable sense of the word.

[44] 294 U. S. 317 (1935).

[45] 294 U. S. 240 (1935).

[46] That is, gold dollars of 25.8 grains, 9/10 fine.

[47] 294 U. S. 330 (1935).

[48] That is, gold dollars of 25.8 grains, 9/10 fine.

[49] 4 Wheat. 316 (1819).

[50] There is some evidence that the courts have not understood the meaning of lawful money. This is discussed on pages 101-104.

[51] *McCulloch v. Maryland,* 4 Wheat. 316 (1819).

[52] *Veazie Bank v. Fenno,* 8 Wall. 533 (1869).

[53] *First National Bank v. Fellows,* 244 U. S. 416 (1917).

[54] Rinehart J. Swenson, "The Supreme Court and the Power of Congress to Regulate Money," *Money and the Law* (New York University School of Law, New York, 1945), p. 26.

[55] Samuel McKee, Jr., ed., *Hamilton's Papers on Public Credit, Commerce and Finance* (Columbia University Press, New York, 1930), p. 123.

[56] 4 Wheat. 316 (1819).

[57] 2 Mason 1 (1819).

[58] 51 U. S. 190 (1850).

[59] *Bush v. Shipman et al.,* 5 Ill. 186 (1843); *Wise Brothers v. Rogers,* 24 Gratt. (Va.) 169 (1873); *Briscoe et al. v. Bank of Kentucky,* 11 Peters 257 (1837).

[60] The various qualities of national bank notes are discussed on pages 85-86.

[61] 13 *Statutes at Large* 99.

[62] Text of this provision is given on pages 96, n. 46.

[63] *Craig v. Missouri,* 4 Peters 410 (1830).

[64] 11 Peters 257 (1857).

[65] C. 47, s. 24.

[66] *Bank of Niagara et al. v. Roosevelt et al.,* 9 Cowen (N. Y.) 409 (1827); *Abbott et al. v. Agricultural Bank of Mississippi,* 19 Miss. 405 (1848); *Dunlap v. Smith et al.,* 12 Ill. 399 (1851); *American Bank v. Wall,* 56 Me. 167 (1868); *Railey et al. v. Bacon et al* 26 Miss., 455 (1853).

[67] 5 Peters 641 (1831).

chapter

3

**LEGAL QUALITIES OF MONEY:
HISTORY AND DEVELOPMENT PRIOR TO
THE ADOPTION OF THE CONSTITUTION**

RUDIMENTARY LEGAL QUALITIES OF MONEY

RUDIMENTARY EXAMPLES OF THE USE OF THE QUALITIES OF legal tender, lawful money, and money receivable for specified purposes may be found in the history of America prior to 1789. With a relatively primitive system of money and credit, it is not surprising that the qualities were much less important at that time than they were to become subsequently. Some of the principles of legal tender and of money receivable for specified purposes are deducible from the terms applied to non-metallic commodities, paper money, and coins in the Colonies, and in the states under the Articles of Confederation. Some use of the words "lawful money" during this period indicates the way in which the phrase eventually came to be employed in legislation.

NON-METALLIC COMMODITIES

The monetary laws of the American Colonies contain numerous examples of non-metallic commodities which were legal tender, or receivable for specified purposes, such as in payments to the public treasuries. A widespread scarcity of gold and silver coin, continuing well into the eighteenth century in most Colonies, forced the colonists to experiment with other media of exchange. Colonial assemblies turned first to those commodities which, by common consent, were in use as substitutes for metallic money. *Wampum,* a type of shell bead used by the Indian tribes for trading purposes, was adopted as money by some colonies.[1] Beaver skins, moose skins, tobacco, and grains of several kinds were used in others. In the Massachusetts Bay Colony corn was a generic term used to describe various grains, or even peas, which passed from hand to hand as media of exchange. In 1628, for example, the customary payment to a surveyor for running the lines of a lot was a peck of corn.[2]

All the commodities used as media of exchange were either

legal tender or receivable in payments of all kinds to the public treasuries at one time or another. Only a few examples need be given here. An exhaustive description would be highly repetitive, and would yield little additional information.[3]

Monetary historians seem to agree that the first legal tender law for non-metallic commodity money in the American Colonies was passed in 1631. In that year the governor and assistants of Massachusetts Bay Colony ordered that "corne shall passe for payment of all debts at the usuall rate it is sold for, except money or beaver be expressly named."[4] Tobacco was legal tender in Virginia[5] from 1647 to 1661.[6] New France made wheat legal tender at specified rates in 1679, and moose skins in 1684.[7]

Many commodities were made receivable by the colonial treasurers in payments of all kinds. In Pennsylvania various kinds of produce were thus received in 1719, and made legal tender at market prices in 1722.[8] North Carolina, in 1715, made seventeen different commodities receivable for taxes at rates specified by the assembly.[9] The same law provided that the commodities could also be used to pay private debts at rates mutually determined by debtor and creditor.

Colonial practice also provides a rudimentary example of the principle of providing for a subsidiary currency by limiting the legal tender quality. For example, in 1635 the Massachusetts Bay Colony ordered that musket balls of full bore should "pass currantly for a farthing a peece, provided that noe man be compelled to take above 12d. att a tyme of them."[10] In 1643, wampum was legal tender up to forty shillings in one payment.[11]

The legal effect of refusing legal tender commodity money differed from that of the present day, and varied from Colony to Colony. The most common practice was to allow two parties to a contract to determine the quality and price of the commodities which were to be used to discharge the debt. If they failed to agree, the issue was referred to an umpire.

Jamaica, for example, made several items of produce legal tender, but set no fixed rates. The value of each commodity used was decided in the individual case by the churchwardens of the parish. Tobacco was legal tender in Maryland in 1713. If the creditor refused the tobacco proffered, the debtor was empowered to request a justice of the peace to appoint two judges or assessors of the value of the tobacco. These judges decided whether or not the value of the tobacco offered was sufficient to discharge the debt. If they decided affirmatively, the creditor was obliged either to accept it or surrender his claim on the debtor.[12]

The commodities which served as money, and which were made legal tender, were not chosen consciously as standard money but as a temporary medium of exchange because of the scarcity of coin. They served some of the other functions of money, too, such as a storehouse of value, more or less imperfectly. Most of the commodities were acceptable within a narrow range, but they lacked homogeneity, durability, and scarcity. In short, they lacked those qualities which are essential to a good standard money. From time to time, the use of commodities as currency seems to have induced production beyond the capacity of the markets to absorb, and to have increased the precariousness of prices in general.

There is no evidence to indicate that the commodities were used as money or made legal tender because they were cheap,[13] or because they were plentiful, or had other uses, such as decoration or edibility. Nor does there seem to be any evidence that making the commodities legal tender appreciably maintained or increased their value, either as money or as commodities. In almost every case there is evidence that the commodities were made legal tender in order to settle legal questions, such as those involving debts, when payment by means of metallic money was almost impossible.

For the most part, the commodities made legal tender were already being used as media of exchange. Legal recognition reaffirmed the judgment of the market place. The characteristic most frequently observed of commodities made legal tender was their general acceptability *without* the legal tender quality.

Experience with legal tender, non-metallic commodities in the Colonies reveals an important principle: that safeguards are necessary to prevent the operation of Gresham's Law when the standard money does not circulate. The poorer grades of the commodity were used most frequently as money while the better grades sought the market. Because of the difficulties and the expense involved in transportation, prices in terms of commodities varied widely from place to place. Prices also varied depending upon the particular medium offered. Prices in terms of commodities with a large export market value tended to be lower than prices in terms of commodities consumed locally.

COLONIAL BILLS OF CREDIT

Massachusetts Bay Colony issued paper money bills of credit in 1690 to pay for a military expedition against the French at Quebec. They were paid at face value to the veterans of the expedition, and to the dependents of those who were casualties. Recipients were compelled by circumstances to accept them, not because of law, but because they were either unable or unwilling to wait until sufficient taxes were collected to pay them. The bills were made receivable by the Treasurer of the Colony in all payments, but there was no direct or indirect compulsion for private persons to accept them in trade or in discharge of private obligations.[14]

Because of the similarity to subsequent provisions of federal statutes, the wording of the bills is of interest. A typical bill reads: "This indented bill for ten shillings due from the Massachusetts colony to the Possessor, shall be in Value equal to Money, and shall be accordingly accepted by the Treasurer, and receivers subordinate to him, in all public payments, and for any stock[15] at any time in the Treasury. Boston, in New England, December 10, 1690."

In 1692 several changes were made in the legal qualities of the bills. They were made receivable by the Treasurer in the payment of taxes at five percent above their face value. A ten-shilling bill, for example, would pay ten and a half shillings in taxes. After being paid in for taxes, the bills were not destroyed but were reissued at par value. They were also made full legal tender. If a creditor refused to accept them, the debtor was discharged of his obligation. This is a more severe penalty than exists at present, but was a common penalty for refusing legal tender bills of credit of various Colonies at this time.[16]

Massachusetts' bills of credit were maintained very nearly at par with English silver coins for several years following 1692. Some students have concluded that the legal tender quality was responsible. A more accurate interpretation seems to be that sufficient advantage was given to the bills by the five percent advance in face value when paid to the Treasurer to maintain them near par. Taxes for redeeming the bills were repeatedly postponed, and new emissions were undertaken. They depreciated steadily to £140 paper for £100 silver in 1716.[17]

These notes or bills were one of the first American issues of paper money. The main purpose seems to have been to increase the revenue of the government by borrowing in anticipation of taxes.

Massachusetts' bills of credit served as a precedent for similar issues in other Colonies. Some were full legal tender, some merely receivable in payments to the various Treasurers. Connecticut, New York, and Rhode Island all emitted similar bills between 1708 and 1750.[18]

Some of these bills also illustrate the use of the legal tender quality to favor debtors as against creditors. Horace White quotes a passage from a letter of the period (dated 1743) concerning Rhode Island's bills of credit: " ' . . . This expedient of depreciating their Government bills, by their laws made a Tender and Currency, is promoted by the fraudulent Debtors and desperate part of the Colony in order to pay former contracts with a much less value than was contracted for and more especially to defraud British merchants in their outstanding debts.' " [19]

The penalties for refusing legal tender paper money in payment of a debt, or for charging more for services, goods or lands in paper than in coin were severe. Not only was the debt extinguished in some of the Colonies, but often the offender's goods were confiscated, or he was imprisoned.[20]

After 1763, the Colonies were specifically forbidden to issue paper money legal tender, and even the bills made receivable for taxes and other public payments were frowned upon and discouraged by the English parliament.[21]

Under certain circumstances, however, such as war, bills of

credit receivable in payments to the Treasurers were permitted. Parliament and the colonial assemblies thus avoided the implication of forcing the acceptance of the bills on those unwilling to take them. The full legal consequence of making the bills legal tender was thus avoided, while still providing a medium of exchange for those who wished to use it.

Whether the principle was realized or not, it provided a legal precedent which was later followed in federal legislation. In those Colonies where the bills were issued sparingly, when taxes were levied for redeeming them, and when the bills were destroyed as redeemed, they seem to have functioned fairly well as a medium of exchange, whether or not they were legal tender.

CONTINENTAL CURRENCY

With reference to legal tender, the experience with Continental Currency was similar to the experience of the Massachusetts Bay Colony with paper money bills of credit in 1690. At first the Continental Currency was not legal tender, but was made receivable by the states in payment of taxes levied by the states. The tax program proposed by the Continental Congress to the states was to extend over four years, beginning November 30, 1779.[22] Depreciation, in terms of specie, became more and more pronounced during the two years following the initial issue of June, 1775. On January 14, 1777, the Continental Congress passed a resolution requesting the legislatures of the several states to declare the Continental Currency a legal tender.[23] All thirteen states complied.

Details of the subsequent depreciation of the Continental Currency are available in most treatises on American financial history.[24] By 1780, repudiation was recognized as inevitable, and Congress recommended that the states repeal their legal tender laws.[25] By 1781, the Continental Currency had ceased to function as a medium of exchange, and thereafter sold in the same manner as a speculative commodity at 99.5 to 99.9 percent discount.[26] Pelatiah Webster observed, "Thus fell, ended and died, the Continental Currency, aged 6 years, the most powerful state engine, and the greatest prodigy of revenue and of the most mysterious, uncontrollable and most magical operation ever known or heard of in the political world. . . . "[27] The death rattle, apparently, was its acceptance in subscriptions to the public debt at 100 to 1 under the refunding act of 1790.

PAPER MONEY OF STATES

The states also issued paper money. In every case it was made full legal tender. Sometimes the legal tender quality applied only to money issued by that state or by the Continental Congress. More often the state made the paper money of other states legal tender as well.[28]

Depreciation of state paper money was similar to that experienced by the Continental Currency, although the extent of the depreciation varied from state to state.

Penalties for refusing legal tender paper money were stringent. They were positive penalties, for the most part, and became increasingly severe as the extent of the depreciation increased. The Rhode Island legislature, for example, made both Rhode Island's paper money and the Continental Currency legal tender in 1775. A person refusing to accept the paper money at face value was publicly declared to be an enemy of his country.[29] Later the penalty was increased to discharging the debt, and in some states the offender was fined, imprisoned, or had his ears cut off.[30]

The experience with Continental Currency and state paper money under the Articles of Confederation serves to illustrate several principles.

First, the major purpose in making the paper money legal tender and receivable for specified purposes was not to establish a monetary standard, but to provide a medium of exchange and of payment. A secondary purpose was to increase government revenues. All of the paper money promised payment in gold, silver, or some specific coin, such as Spanish milled dollars. Although this turned out to be little more than a pious hope, it indicates that the *standard* moneys were gold and silver.

Second, safeguards for the protection of the standard money were not employed. The legal tender quality was repeatedly extended, not limited, and positive penalties were severe. In practice, there was no effective limitation on the amount of the money issued, and no methods for retiring it were adopted. Finally, either because the legislators were unable or unwilling to do so, no provisions were made for the conversion of the paper money into the standard money. The effect, but not the intent, was to adopt an inconvertible paper money standard which eventually resulted in monetary chaos and repudiation.

Third, the experience indicates the inability of the legal tender quality to maintain or preserve the purchasing power value of money. The most severe penalties for advancing prices, the price-fixing enactments, and the prohibition of barter all failed to prevent depreciation.

Fourth, two other purposes were evident in making the paper money legal tender. One was to obtain revenue for the government regardless of the effect upon either debtors or creditors. The other was to favor debtors. The results of the latter motive do not recommend it. The excesses indulged in by debtor-paper money parties in many states in their efforts to favor debtors resulted in the express prohibition of the issue of bills of credit by the states in the Federal Constitution.

NOTES OF BANKS

The act of the Continental Congress chartering the Bank of North America in 1781 made the notes of the bank receivable in payments to the state Treasuries, and in payments to the Continental Treasury. Article XII of the Bank's charter provides that the notes of the bank shall be "receivable in payment of the duties and taxes of every state in the Union, and from the respective states by the Treasury of the United States."[31] This relationship of the Bank's notes to the government of the Confederation continued until 1787, when the Bank reopened under a new charter received from the State of Pennsylvania.

The notes of the Bank of North America survived the monetary chaos of the Revolutionary War, and were accepted at par with gold and silver coins. Continental Currency depreciated against specie and did not survive.

This comparison illustrates the importance of safeguarding standard money. The notes of the Bank were not legal tender, but were receivable in the payments specified in the Bank's charter. They were redeemable in specie on demand at the bank, and their issue was limited by the conservative lending policy of the Bank's officers.

COINS

English coins were legal tender by virtue of the superior authority of parliament to that of the Colonial assemblies. Sometimes the Colonies unlawfully made foreign coins a legal tender as well. English, Dutch, French and Spanish gold and silver coins were made legal tender in the Colonies and in the states under the Articles of Confederation after the repudiation of the Continental Currency.

The scarcity of coin was so great that a study of the qualities of various coins reveals little. Even when worn smooth, or clipped, the coins seem to have been readily acceptable. Some Colonies appear to have made foreign coins legal tender at an increased rate over their value in terms of English coins in an effort to prevent their export. Massachusetts and Connecticut made Dutch gold ducatoons legal tender in 1642[32] and Spanish silver pieces of eight in 1647,[33] at rates in excess of the English coin equivalent.

Massachusetts was the only Colony to attempt to establish a mint. The mint opened in 1651, and the shillings issued from it were less valuable in terms of silver than English silver shillings. Massachusetts made the coins legal tender at their nominal value, however, in the hope of preventing exportation.[34]

"PROCLAMATION MONEY" AND "LAWFUL MONEY"

In 1685, the Massachusetts mint was forced to close by the

parliament in London.[35] In 1703, parliament issued a proclamation naming the rates at which the various coins, Massachusetts and foreign, would be valued in terms of English money.[36] The valuation approximated that of full weight English coins.

The existence of two different sets of rates, one in the proclamation of parliament, the other in the acts of the Colonies, gave rise to a widespread popular nomenclature of "proclamation money" and "lawful money." "Proclamation money" meant English coin of full weight, or the equivalent, while "lawful money" meant coins valued at the Colonial rates.[37] The term "lawful money" came to mean any gold and silver coin in popular usage regardless of whether the coins were English or foreign. No appreciable amount of full weight English coin circulated. When prices were stated in terms of "lawful money" gold or silver coin was intended (chiefly silver), and without regard to the legal tender qualities of the coins.

This is illustrated by a lawsuit on a promissory note, dated June 16, 1778, calling for payment in "lawful money." The court interpreted this to mean silver coin, and observed that this usage was widely recognized in the State of Connecticut.[38] Similar use of the words seems to have been common in Rhode Island.[39]

ORIGIN OF LAWFUL MONEY

Bills of credit of Rhode Island afford the first use of the term "lawful money," in the technical sense, that the author has been able to find. After 1756, bills of credit issued by the Rhode Island Colony were made payable in silver, in two years from the date of issue, in silver at 6s. 8d. per ounce, or its equivalent in gold. This seems to have been the colonial rate for an ounce of silver, and not the English "proclamation" rate. By popular usage, they were called "lawful money bills" to indicate the type of money in which they were to be redeemed.[40] This indicates one way in which the term "lawful money," in the technical sense, found its way into legislative vocabularies.

There seems to be no evidence that the legal tender quality had anything to do with the term "lawful money bills." They were legal tender at times, and not at others. Bills which were legal tender, but did not have the clause concerning redemption in silver, were never called "lawful money bills." The fact that these bills were never redeemed does not seem to destroy the validity of the argument that the words "lawful money" were used to designate the *kind* of money intended to be used in redeeming them.

FOOTNOTES

1 Condy Raguet, *A Treatise on Currency and Banking* (Grigg and Elliott, Philadelphia, 1839), p. 175.

2 J. B. Felt, *An Historical Account of Massachusetts Currency* (Perkins and Marvin, Boston, 1839), p. 14; Curtis P. Nettels, *The Money Supply in the American Colonies before 1720* (University of Wisconsin Press, Madison, Wis., 1934), p. 209.

3 Rather full descriptions of the various kinds and characteristics of these commodity moneys may be found in William Ridgeway, *The Origin of Metallic Currency and Weight Standards* (University Press, Cambridge, Mass., 1892), and in Raguet, *op. cit.*

4 Sophonisba P. Breckinridge, *Legal Tender: A Study in British and American Monetary History* (University of Chicago Press, Chicago, 1903), p. 53; Felt, *op. cit.,* p. 16. Raguet, *op. cit.,* p. 175, mentions, without citation, a Virginia law of 1618 making tobacco legal tender at three shillings per pound.

5 "Pass current in the payment of debts" is the phrase used—similar to the English practice at the time.

6 Raguet, *op. cit.,* pp. 176-177; Horace White, *Money and Banking* (Ginn and Company, Boston, 1895), p. 6.

7 R. M. Breckenridge, "The Paper Currencies of New France," *Journal of Political Economy* (1893), Vol. I, p. 409.

8 Henry Phillips, *Historical Sketches of the Currency of the American Colonies prior to the Adoption of the Federal Constitution* (W. E. Woodward, Roxbury, Mass., 1865-66), Vol. I, pp. 12-13.

9 Charles J. Bullock, *Essays on the Monetary History of the United States* (The Macmillan Company, New York, 1900), pp. 125-126.

10 Felt, *op. cit.,* p. 16.

11 Henry Bronson, *A Historical Account of Connecticut Currency, Continental Currency and the Finances of the Revolution* (New Haven Historical Society, New Haven, 1865), p. 4.

12 Nettels, *op. cit.,* p. 211n. The laws of Virginia in 1666 operated similarly according to White, *op. cit.,* p. 9.

13 Richard A. Lester in *Monetary Experiments: Early American and Recent Scandinavian* (Princeton University Press, Princeton, 1939), p. 12, expresses the belief that commodities were used in an effort to

obtain a cheap, economical money which could serve two purposes: as a decoration, or as an edible substance, and as a medium of exchange. This seems to overlook entirely the fundamental characteristic of acceptability, and fails to differentiate long-run and temporary forces determining the adoption of a monetary standard. The factor of cheapness, moreover, is of no apparent significance. There were a multitude of things cheaper than the ones chosen as money.

14 Felt, *op. cit.,* pp. 50-52.
15 That is, specie—particularly silver coin.
16 Further details concerning the bills of credit during the period 1690 to 1750 may be obtained from Felt, *op. cit.,* pp. 50-55; White, *op. cit.,* pp. 120-121; Bronson, *op. cit.,* p. 28; and Davis R. Dewey, *Financial History of the United States* (Longmans, Green and Company, New York, 1934), pp. 20-23.
17 A. McFarland Davis, *Currency and Banking in the Province of Massachusetts Bay* (American Economic Association, Evanston, Ill., 1901), Vol. I, p. 89.
18 Bullock, *op. cit.,* p. 207; Elisha R. Potter, *Some Account of the bills of credit or paper money of Rhode Island* (J. E. Brown, Providence, R. I., 1865), p. 7.
19 White, *op. cit.,* p. 124.
20 Potter, *op. cit.,* pp. 18, 32-33; White, *op. cit.,* p. 127.
21 13 Geo. III, c. 57. This act is described in detail on page 21.
22 *Journals of Congress* (1775), Vol. I, p. 174.
23 *Journals of Congress* (1777), Vol. III, p. 20.
24 Dewey, *op. cit.,* Chap. II; Phillips, *op. cit.,* Vol. II, *passim.* The outstanding contemporary description is that of Pelatiah Webster in *Political Essays on the Nature and Operation of Money, Public Finances and other Subjects* (Joseph Crukshank, Philadelphia, 1791).
25 *Journals of Congress* (1780), Vol. VI, p. 48.
26 Dewey, *op. cit.,* p. 41.
27 Webster, *op. cit.,* p. 175.
28 Bullock, *op. cit.,* p. 264; Felt, *op. cit.,* p. 174; Phillips, *op. cit.,* Vol. II, pp. 79, 145.
29 Phillips, *op. cit.,* Vol. II, p. 30.
30 White, *op. cit.,* p. 139.
31 *Journals of Congress* (1781) Vol. VII, p. 108.
32 Felt, *op. cit.,* p. 26; Bronson, *op. cit.,* p. 14.
33 Davis, *op. cit.,* p. 38.
34 Felt, *op. cit.,* pp. 31-33, 41.
35 *Ibid.,* p. 48.
36 *Ibid.,* pp. 58-59.
37 Davis, *op. cit.,* pp. 25-30.
38 *Dorrance v. Stewart,* 1 Yeates (Pa.) 349 (1791).
39 Potter, *op. cit.,* p. 112.
40 Bronson, *op. cit.,* p. 111.

chapter

4

LEGAL QUALITIES OF MONEY: HISTORY AND DEVELOPMENT, 1789 TO 1862

THE HISTORY OF LEGAL QUALITIES OF MONEY UNDER THE
Constitution may be divided conveniently into two periods—
before and after 1862. In 1862, for the first time, the United
States issued an irredeemable legal tender paper money, specifically designated lawful money, the result of which was to introduce a considerable amount of confusion and complications into
our monetary history.

A

LEGAL TENDER

Coins alone were legal tender prior to 1862, and the coins
were so designated only by act of Congress. The chief purpose
of legal tender laws during this period was to provide a means
of payment, capable of settling legal questions arising out of
exchange, contracts, and other deferred payments. There is no
evidence that coins were made legal tender for other purposes
such as favoring debtors or creditors as a class, or in order to
provide revenue for the government.

LEGISLATION CONCERNING THE
MONETARY STANDARD

All federal statutes defining the standard money, and providing for coinage, contain a clause designating the standard
coins legal tender. The first coinage act under the Constitution
of the United States (April 2, 1792) defined the dollar in terms
of weight and fineness of both gold and silver, provided for the
construction and operation of a mint, and authorized the issue
of gold, silver and copper coins. Section 16 of the act stated:
"... All the gold and silver coins which shall have been
struck at, and issued from the said Mint, shall be a lawful tender

in all payments whatsoever, those of full weight according to the values hereinbefore declared, and those of less than full weight at values proportional to their respective weights."[1]

With the exception of a change in the words "lawful tender" to "legal tender," this wording is typical of all coinage acts to 1862, and will be found in all coinage acts referring to the standard moneys. The actual wording varies only slightly, and the meaning remains unchanged.

A slight alteration of the weight and fineness of the standard gold coins took place in 1834,[2] and a change in the fineness of gold and silver coins took place in 1837.[3] The new coins authorized were declared to be legal tender, but nothing was said concerning the legal tender quality of the coins previously issued. Legal tender at face value when of full weight continued to be a quality of the coins issued before the alterations of the standard moneys in 1834 and 1837. Additional gold coins were authorized by the Act of March 3, 1849, and were similarly declared to be legal tender.[4]

The circumstances surrounding these changes in the monetary standard are of some historical interest. The alteration of the gold coins, particularly the law of 1834, provided a precedent for the decision of the Supreme Court concerning the constitutionality of the United States notes issued in 1862.

From 1792 to 1834 silver coins were the principal part of the media of exchange. Over most of the period, gold appears to have been relatively more valuable as bullion than as coin. Since both gold and silver coins were legal tender, contracts expressed in terms of dollars could be discharged by the payment of either gold or silver coin. Silver coin was commonly used because it was received more often, and because payment in gold coin meant a slightly higher payment in terms of market value of the metals.

In the decision which upheld Congress' power to issue legal tender paper money, the Supreme Court rejected the contention that such an issue violated the obligation of contracts. Among other reasons, the Court argued that the obligation of contracts had been impaired in 1834, and that no question had been raised concerning the power of Congress to do so. The court said:

"The creditor who had a thousand dollars due him July 31, 1834, the day before the act took effect, was entitled to one thousand dollars of coined gold of the weight and fineness of the then existing coinage. The day after, he was entitled only to a sum 6 percent less in weight and in market value, or to a smaller number of silver dollars."[5]

This statement is not accurate. Payment could have been made with the same number of silver coins both before and after the act. The option to pay in either gold or silver rested with the debtor, and to argue that the obligation of contracts was appreciably changed is patently erroneous. The act was no more than a readjustment of legal values to market values characteristic of a bimetallic standard. Apparently the Court failed to distinguish between such an alteration of relative rates under a bimetallic standard and the adoption of an inconvertible paper standard. Judges often have been better lawyers than economists.

FOREIGN COINS

The Act of February 9, 1793, made specific foreign coins "a legal tender for the payment of all debts and demands" at rates approximately proportional to their gold and silver content in terms of the coins authorized to be issued by the Mint.[6] The Mint did not begin operations until October, 1794. Prior to that year, foreign coins were the only coins in use. Even after the coinage operations were begun, foreign coins continued to be an important part of the media of exchange. The legal tender quality of some of these coins was re-enacted at various intervals until the Act of February 21, 1857.[7]

This use of the legal tender quality illustrates the fact that the legal tender quality is important to the medium of exchange, and not necessarily to the standard money. From February, 1793, to October, 1794, the standard gold and silver coins, although legal tender, did not exist in fact. The legal tender quality was given to foreign coins, which were in actual use, in such a way as to assure that the means of measurement would correspond with the standard established in law. As long as the coins struck at the United States mint did not circulate, their legal tender quality was of no consequence whatsoever.

SUBSIDIARY COINAGE

The copper cents and half-cents which had been authorized under the coinage act of 1792 were not made legal tender specifically. Nothing was said about their legal tender quality. Professor Carothers, in his study of our fractional money, says that no one knew, during the succeeding fifty years, whether these cents and half-cents were unlimited legal tender, limited legal tender, or without the quality of legal tender at all.[8] So far as this author has been able to determine, no case involving this question was ever brought before the Supreme Court. At least one state court, however, held that the coins had no legal tender quality whatever.[9]

Numerous suggestions to limit the legal tender quality of subsidiary silver coins appear to have been made from time to time after 1820,[10] but the first limitation did not occur until March 3, 1851.[11] This act reduced the postage rate for letters from five to three cents per ounce, and provided for the coinage of a three-cent piece to be "a legal tender in payment of all debts for all sums of thirty cents and under."[12]

This was the first time that a silver coin had been issued with less silver content than that proportional to its nominal part of a silver dollar, and the first use of the limited legal tender quality in subsidiary coins.[13]

This principle of limiting the legal tender quality of fractional silver and other subsidiary coins was extended in 1853.[14] Weights of the coins were reduced, and their legal tender quality was limited to five dollars in one payment. The Act of February 12, 1873, later limited the legal tender quality of non-silver minor coins to twenty-five cents in one payment.[15]

Fractional coins appear to have been made legal tender to facilitate the use of them in small payments and the fractional parts of larger ones. The legal tender quality was limited to prevent making large payments in small coins in order to annoy or inconvenience the payee. After the laws recognized the limited legal tender principle, the payee could refuse to accept large numbers of small coins without prejudice.

B
MONEY RECEIVABLE FOR SPECIFIED PURPOSES

Foreign coins, Treasury notes, and notes of banks were made receivable for specified purposes from 1789 to 1862. The purposes of making money receivable seems to have been to give a limited legal recognition to such money while avoiding the legal consequence of the full legal tender quality. A secondary purpose was to facilitate the borrowing of money. Most frequently during this period, money was made receivable in specified payments to governments, such as the payment of taxes.

FOREIGN COINS

Some of the foreign gold coins, which at first had been legal tender by the provisions of the Act of February 9, 1793, were no longer made legal tender under the Act of March 3, 1823. Instead they were made receivable in payment for lands purchased from the United States.

These coins, although they had been legal tender and were rather widely circulated, appear to have become worn and clipped. Making them receivable in payment of lands purchased from the United States, instead of legal tender, served two purposes: (1) it avoided any pressure upon individuals to accept underweight or worn coins, if they were unwilling to do so; and (2) it tended to attract the coins to the government for recoinage into American full weight coins, thus improving the quality of the coinage in general.

TREASURY NOTES

Evidences of the debt of the United States have been made

receivable in payments to the United States, and have served as a part of the media of exchange. In 1797, evidences of the funded debt of the United States were made receivable by the Treasury in the purchases of public lands.[16] In later years, partly to secure revenue, partly to supplement the existing media of exchange, Treasury notes were made receivable in all payments to the government of the United States.

The first issue of these Treasury notes was authorized by the Act of June 30, 1812.[17] They matured one year from the date of issue, could not be reissued, were payable to order, and transferable on delivery and assignment. The act stated that the notes "shall be receivable in payments of all duties and taxes laid by authority of the United States and of all public lands sold by the said authority." Similar issues were authorized in 1813, 1814, and 1815. The denominations of the first three issues were stated in the acts; the fourth issue was in denominations set at the discretion of the Secretary of the Treasury. All four paid interest at the rate of 5.4 percent per year.

A resolution to make these Treasury notes legal tender was submitted to the House of Representatives on November 12, 1814. By a vote of 95 to 45, the resolution was rejected. During the debate, the following objections were made to a consideration of the resolution: (1) that Congress could not make the notes legal tender within the powers granted to it by the Constitution; (2) that it was unnecessary to make them legal tender for the purposes at hand; and (3) that it would be unjust to force them upon a creditor who did not wish to accept them.[18]

It seems clear that the Congress made the notes receivable in payments to the government in order to avoid the implications of full legal tender. They did circulate, however, and were an important part of the media of exchange until 1816.

Congress authorized another issue of Treasury notes in 1837. The purposes again were to provide revenue to the government, and to provide a medium of exchange.[19]

State chartered banks had suspended specie payments during the financial panic of 1837, and receipts by the Treasury fell off sharply. In authorizing the issue, the Treasury sought to borrow temporarily in order to meet a deficit, and to provide a currency in which the Treasury's revenues could be collected. Like the previous issues, they were receivable for all dues and taxes to the government and for the purchase of public lands. The power to reissue, which had not been granted previously, was added on May 21, 1838.[20] Similar issues were authorized in 1839, 1840, 1841, 1842, 1843, 1847, 1857, and 1860.

An Act of July 17, 1861, authorized the issuance of these Treasury notes in small denominations, maturing and bearing interest at the discretion of the Secretary of the Treasury. The main purpose seems to have been to provide revenue for the Treasury. The legislation was adopted so hastily that nothing was said about the notes being receivable in payments to the United States.[21] This provision was added by the Act of August 5, 1861.[22]

Prior to 1862, seventeen authorizations were made by Congress for the issuance of Treasury notes, receivable in all payments to the United States. This device allowed the Treasury to borrow money in anticipation of taxes, supplied a medium of exchange other than coin or bank notes, and yet avoided the consequences of issuing legal tender paper money.

If the notes had been legal tender, without providing for convertibility into the standard moneys on demand, they might have become a paper currency which private individuals would have been under some pressure to accept, whether they wished to do so or not. The legal tender quality might have reduced the willingness of subsequent legislatures to provide for their retirement, or retirement might have been delayed. By the expedient of making the notes receivable in payments to the government, the possible consequences of full legal tender paper money were avoided, while still satisfying the purposes of their issue.

NOTES OF THE FIRST AND SECOND BANKS OF THE UNITED STATES

Section 10 of the charter of the First Bank of the United States, passed by Congress on February 25, 1792, made the notes of the bank receivable in all payments to the United States. The act provided that " . . . the bills or notes of the said corporation originally made payable, or which shall become payable, on demand, in gold or silver coin, shall be receivable in all payments to the United States."[23]

An identical provision was contained in the charter of the Second Bank of the United States, but with the additional qualifying clause, "unless otherwise directed by Act of Congress."[24]

Notes of these banks were thus made receivable in all payments to the United States on condition that the notes were paid in gold and silver coin on demand. The Treasury notes, on the other hand, were receivable unconditionally. The purpose of the legislators appears to have been to encourage the use of bank notes as a medium of exchange, but to insure payment in legal tender coin on demand, thus providing a check upon the activities of the banking corporations. This conditional clause does not reappear in subsequent legislation making other bank notes receivable in payments to the United States.

THE "SPECIE CIRCULAR" OF 1836

On July 11, 1836, Secretary of the Treasury Woodbury, under President Andrew Jackson, directed the receivers of the public money to accept nothing but gold or silver coin in payment for public lands and for taxes.[25] At that time there was still in force a joint resolution of April 30, 1816, which listed the moneys which would be accepted by the government's agents.[26] These included (1) "legal currency of the United States";[27] (2) Treasury notes; (3) notes of the Bank of the United States; and (4) "notes of specie paying banks."

Although the question was never decided specifically by the courts, it seems probable, in the light of subsequent decisions by the Supreme Court, that the Specie Circular usurped the authority of the legislature. In its original form it appears to have been in conflict with laws of Congress making Treasury notes and notes of the United States Bank receivable in payments of all kinds to the United States. After a period of experi-

menting with some compromise bills,[28] the law establishing the
Independent Treasury System in 1846 stated explicitly that only
gold and silver coin or Treasury notes would be receivable in
payments to the United States.[29]

MONEY RECEIVABLE FOR SPECIFIED PURPOSES IN
STATE LAWS

All of the states, at one time or another, have designated
bank notes, land warrants, and other things receivable in payment of dues and taxes to the state. Some also ruled explicitly
that bank notes were receivable in all payments to the bank of
issue.[30]

When the money made receivable by state laws was issued
directly by the state, with the obvious purpose of providing a
medium of exchange, these acts appear to have violated the
prohibition upon state issues of bills of credit in the Constitution.[31] When the purpose was merely to indicate the money or
thing which would be accepted by the state in payment of taxes
or other dues, and the money was not issued directly by the
state, the laws did not exceed state authority to indicate the
moneys the state would accept in legitimately exercising its power
to tax. Using the concept of receivability with respect to bank
notes was also a means of regulating banking corporations existing under the authority of the state.

C
LAWFUL MONEY

The origin of the term lawful money appears to center upon
its use to describe gold and silver coin. Lawful money, meaning
gold and silver, gradually came to be used in state laws designating the kind of asset which could be used legally as a reserve
against notes issued by banks chartered by the states.

From 1791 to 1836, legislative attempts to regulate the kind of asset to be held against note issue liabilities apparently did not use the words "lawful money." The legislators often confused an asset and a liability. Restrictions on notes were commonly related to the amount of a bank's capital, apparently on the assumption that the capital consisted of gold or silver and provided a specie reserve.

The charter of the First Bank of the United States, for example, restricted that institution's total debt to 100 percent of its capital "over and above the monies then acually deposited in the bank for safekeeping."[32] A New York rule of thumb, limiting the total amount of a bank's debt, exclusive of deposits, to three times the amount of its capital, appears in bank charters granted from 1800 to 1812.[33]

It seems apparent that the legislators were assuming that these provisions of law established reserves of gold and silver against note obligations of the banks. They assumed that, when a bank was chartered, the capital stock would be purchased with gold and silver, and that upon this as a reserve, a somewhat larger amount in bank notes could be issued. Pelatiah Webster expressed the reasoning clearly: "It is also found by experience, that any sum of money in the stock of a bank well regulated and managed is sufficient to support the credit of double or triple its amount in bank bills, whilst each of these bills is indisputably as good as cash, because the possessor may at any time exchange them at the bank for solid hard money."[34]

This confusion of assets and liabilities resulted in numerous abuses.[35] The technical concept of lawful money dates from the subsequent attempts by state legislatures to regulate the kinds of assets which could be held legally by banking institutions as a reserve against note and deposit liabilities.

LEGISLATION, 1837 TO 1862

A Virginia law of 1837 entitled "An Act establishing general regulations for the incorporation of banks" apparently contained the first modern use of lawful money in the technical sense. The law stated:

". . . The total amount of bills or notes of any bank in circulation shall not at any time exceed five times the amount of *gold and silver coin of the lawful money of the United States,* the actual property and in the possession of the bank, and held to pay the demands against it. And whenever, in consequence of the gold and silver coin, as aforesaid, being drawn from the bank in payment of the demands against it or otherwise, it shall so happen that the amount of gold and silver coin, as aforesaid, shall be reduced to less than one-fifth of its said bills and notes in circulation, the said bank shall make no new loan or discount, until by curtailment or otherwise, its gold and silver coin as aforesaid shall bear to its said bills and notes in circulation, a greater proportion than one-fifth."[36]

Similarly, a New York law of 1838, entitled "An Act to authorize the business of banking," uses the words "lawful money of the United States" and "specie" interchangeably to indicate the kind of money to be used for redeeming the circulating notes of banks incorporated under the law. Paragraph 4 of the Act reads: "In case the maker or makers of any such circulating note countersigned and registered as aforesaid, shall at any time hereafter, on lawful demand during the usual hours of business, between the hours of ten and three o'clock, at the place where such note is payable, fail or refuse to redeem such note in the lawful money of the United States, the holder of such note making such demand may cause the same to be protested for non-payment. . . ."

Paragraph 33, which defines the kind and amount of the reserve to be held by the bank against its notes in circulation, uses the word "specie" instead of "lawful money of the United States." This paragraph reads: "No association of persons authorized to carry on the business of banking under this act, shall at any time, for the space of twenty days, have on hand at their place of business, less than twelve and a half per cent in specie, on the amount of the bills or notes in circulation as money."[37]

From 1837 to 1860 similar laws were passed by all the state legislatures. Some used the words "lawful money," some "specie," some "gold and silver coin." The intent and purpose in each case were similar, if not identical, to the Virginia and New York statutes.

The accompanying table summarizes the percentage and kind of reserve required under the various state laws. The significant feature of this period is the tendency to use the words "lawful money" to define the *kind* of asset of which the reserve might be composed. The liability against which this lawful money was held usually consisted of notes outstanding alone, although some laws combined both note and deposit liabilities.

RESERVE REQUIREMENTS IN STATE LAWS
1837 TO 1860

State	Year	Percent	Kind of liability	Kind of asset to be held
Virginia[38]	1837	20	note issue	lawful money, gold and silver
Georgia[39]	1838	25	note issue	gold and silver coin, lawful money
New York[40]	1838	12½	note issue	specie, lawful money
Ohio[41]	1839	33	cash responsibilities	gold and silver, lawful money
Louisiana[42]	1842	33	note issue	specie
Connecticut[43]	1848	10	note issue	lawful money of United States
Indiana[44]	1853	12½	note issue	gold and silver coin, lawful money

Missouri[45]	1857	33	note issue	specie
Maine[46]	1858	5	note issue	gold and silver coin
Massachusetts[47]	1858	15	notes and deposits	specie, gold and silver coin
Pennsylvania[48]	1860	8	note issue	specie, gold and silver coin, lawful money

It is not possible to say, as far as this author has been able to determine, whether gold and silver coin were designated lawful money for reserves of state banks by these laws because of the desirable characteristics of the metals, or whether they were designated lawful money because they were legal tender. Logic and reason makes the former more likely.

The fact is that all gold and silver coins were legal tender to some degree. Prior to 1851, moreover, all gold and silver coins were of full weight. It seems probable that the characteristics of the metal which made them desirable as standard moneys were also desirable characteristics of legal tender and lawful money.

FOOTNOTES

[1] 1 *Statutes at Large* 246.
[2] Act of June 28, 1834, 4 *Statutes at Large* 799. The weight and fineness of the $10 gold piece was changed from 270 grains of gold, 0.916 2/3 fine to 258 grains of gold 0.899225 fine. In terms of pure gold content, this reduced the $10 gold piece from 247.5 grains to 232.0 grains—a reduction of 6.26 percent.
[3] Act of January 18, 1837, 5 *Statutes at Large* 136. The fineness of both gold and silver coins was reduced or increased to nine-tenths (0.9).
[4] 9 *Statutes at Large* 394.
[5] *Knox v. Lee, Parker v. Davis,* 12 Wall. 457 (1870).
[6] 1 *Statutes at Large* 300.
[7] In 1798, 1802, 1806, 1816, 1819, 1821, 1823, 1834, and 1843.

8 Neil Carothers, *Fractional Money* (John Wiley and Sons, Inc., New York, 1930), p. 307.

9 *M'Clarin v. Nesbitt*, 2 Nott. and M'Cord (S.C.) 519 (1820).

10 Carothers, *op. cit.*, pp. 70-76.

11 9 *Statutes at Large* 587.

12 The coins were composed of silver and copper, and weighed 12 3/8 grains gross. Thus the gross weight of 33 1/3 of the coins was equal to the weight of a standard silver dollar (33 1/3 x 12 3/8 = 412½) although the silver weight of this number of coins was considerably less than 412½ grains.

13 The legal tender quality of these three-cent pieces was raised to sixty cents by the Act of March 3, 1865, 13 *Statutes at Large* 517.

14 Act of February 21, 1853, 10 *Statutes at Large* 160.

15 17 *Statutes at Large* 424. The Act of June 9, 1879, subsequently raised the limitation for fractional silver coins to ten dollars in one payment. No other alteration of the legal tender quality of subsidiary coins took place until May 12, 1933. This act is discussed on pages 109-111.

16 1 *Statutes at Large* 507.

17 2 *Statutes at Large* 766.

18 *Annals of Congress,* 13th Cong., 3d Sess., p. 557.

19 5 *Statutes at Large* 201.

20 5 *Statutes at Large* 228.

21 12 *Statutes at Large* 259.

22 12 *Statutes at Large* 313.

23 1 *Statutes at Large* 191.

24 3 *Statutes at Large* 266.

25 *Debates of Congress* (1836) Vol. XIII, pp. 7-8.

26 *Annals of Congress,* 14th Cong., 1st Sess. (1816), p. 1440.

27 That is, gold and silver coin.

28 For example, providing specified proportions of the receipts to be made in coin only; 5 *Statutes at Large* 385.

29 9 *Statutes at Large* 59.

30 The reasons for this type of receivability are discussed on pages 33-35.

31 The authority of the states to issue such bills is discussed on pages 34-38.

32 1 *Statutes at Large* 191. The purpose of this provision is discussed in detail by John T. Holdsworth in *The First Bank of the United States,* U. S. Nat. Mon. Com. Pubs., 61st Cong., 2d Sess., Sen. Doc. No. 571 (Washington, 1910), pp. 29-30.

33 L. C. Root, "New York Bank Currency," *Sound Currency* (New York, 1895), Vol. II, No. 5, p. 2.

34 *An Essay on Credit* (1786) in *Political Essays on the Nature and Operation of Money, Public Finances and other subjects* (Joseph Crukshank, Philadelphia, 1791), p. 436.

35 The abuses are described in detail by R. G. Rodkey in *Legal Reserves*

    in American Banking (Michigan Business Studies, Ann Arbor, 1934), Vol. VI, No. 5.

36 *Acts of the General Assembly of Virginia* (1836-1837), Chap. 82, Sec. 3 (italics supplied).

37 *Laws of New York*, 61st Sess. (1838), Chap. 260.

38 *Laws of Virginia* (1836-1837), Chap. 82, Sec. 3.

39 *Cobb's General Laws of Georgia* (1851), Art. I, Sec. 55.

40 *Laws of New York* (1838), 61st Sess., Chap. 260.

41 *Swan's Statutes of Ohio* (1840), Chap. 15, Sec. 10.

42 *Louisiana Laws* (1841-1842), Act. 22, Sec. 2.

43 *Connecticut Proceedings of the Assembly* (1848), Chap. XVII, Sec. 12.

44 *Revised Statutes of the State of Indiana* (1852), Chap. 10, Sec. 33.

45 *Laws of Missouri* (1856-1857), Art. I, Sec. 37.

46 *Revised Statutes of the State of Maine* (1857), Chap. 47, Sec. 22.

47 *General Statutes of the State of Massachusetts* (1860), Chap. 57, Sec. 19.

48 *Pennsylvania Laws* (1860), No. 376, Sec. 31.

chapter

5

LEGAL QUALITIES OF MONEY: HISTORY AND DEVELOPMENT, 1862 TO 1933

A

LEGAL TENDER

UNITED STATES NOTES

THE ACT OF FEBRUARY 25, 1862, AUTHORIZED THE FIRST issue of legal tender paper money under the Constitution of the United States. The Secretary of the Treasury was empowered to issue $150,000,000 in non-interest-bearing notes, in denominations of not less than five dollars, which were declared to be "receivable in payment of all taxes, internal duties, excises, debts and demands of every kind due to the United States, except duties on imports, and of all claims and demands against the United States of every kind whatsoever, except for interest on bonds and notes, which shall be paid in coin, and shall also be lawful money and a legal tender in payment of all debts, public and private, within the United States, except duties on imports and interest as aforesaid."[1]

Although popularly called "legal tenders" or "greenbacks," these notes were not full legal tender. An examination of the decisions rendered by the Supreme Court reveals that they could not be used to pay duties on imports,[2] to pay taxes to state treasuries if the state laws called for payment in coin,[3] or to pay obligations between private parties where the terms of the contract specified payment in coin or bullion.[4]

The purpose of the act was to provide revenue for the Federal Treasury. The effect of the act was to establish a dual monetary system consisting of gold and silver coin for a select few payments, and an irredeemable paper money for the great majority of payments. For all practical purposes, the monetary standard became irredeemable paper, since there was no provision, direct or indirect, for maintaining the paper currency at a par with the gold and silver dollars.

Gold and silver, for the most part, resembled commodities,

rather than money.[5] Gold, for example, was bought and sold on the New York Stock Exchange in order to obtain the means of paying customs duties, to obtain the means of buying foreign exchange, to speculate, or to seek protection against the depreciation in the purchasing power of the "greenbacks" in much the same way as any commodity might be purchased as a hedge against general price rises. In terms of an index number of wholesale prices, the price level jumped from 100 in 1862 to 185 in 1865. The price of gold, in terms of "greenbacks," fluctuated more frequently and more extensively than the general price level, partly in response to the changing tides of war.

With no change in the legal tender quality of the "greenbacks," they declined in value (in terms of gold) to an average of thirty-nine cents for July and August, 1864, and remained at less than ninety cents until 1876. Thereafter they slowly approached parity with gold, as the Secretary of the Treasury accumulated a redemption fund in gold.[6]

The United States notes from 1862 to 1879 demonstrate that the legal tender quality is not sufficient to assure that the legal standard money will function as such. Although gold and silver coin were the only unlimited legal tender money, a *de facto* paper standard existed. In fact, no change in the legal tender quality of the United States notes occurred until June 17, 1930 (when their acceptance in payment of customs dues was authorized), although several major changes took place in the monetary standard.

THE "CRIME OF 1873"

The Act of February 12, 1873, revised and codified the coinage laws.[7] Gold coins authorized included a one-dollar piece, weighing 25.8 grains of gold, 9/10 fine, and other gold coins in multiples of the one-dollar coin up to a double eagle of twenty dollars. Silver coins included a "trade dollar" weighing 420 grains of standard silver (378 grains of fine silver), and some fractional silver coins. All gold coins were designated full legal tender when not below the legal limit of tolerance in weight, and all the silver coins were designated legal tender up to five dollars in one payment.[8] No provision was made for the coinage of the so-called standard silver dollar of 412½ grains of standard silver, and nothing was said about the legal tender quality of those in existence. This omission later came to be called the "Crime of 1873."

If the omission in 1873 was a "crime," the adoption of the Revised Statutes on June 22, 1874, committed at least a misdemeanor. Section 3585 provided that "silver coins of the United States" would be legal tender up to five dollars in one payment. It would seem that this applied to standard silver dollars coined before 1873, as well as fractional silver coins and trade dollars coined under the authority of the act of 1873.

The "crime," at the time it was "committed," was of little more than academic significance. United States notes and national bank notes were the major part of the media of exchange, and were not redeemable in gold or silver (except for the notes of national gold banks under the Act of July 12, 1870). Both gold and silver coins were at premiums in terms of "greenbacks."

BLAND-ALLISON ACT OF 1878

The Act of February 28, 1878, popularly called the Bland-Allison Act, authorized the Secretary of the Treasury to purchase not less than $2,000,000 nor more than $4,000,000 of silver each month, and to coin the silver into silver dollars of 412½ grains of standard silver (371¼ grains of fine silver).[9] The silver dollars thus coined were declared to be "legal tender except where otherwise expressly stated in the contract."[10] Provision was also made for the issuance of silver certificates in exchange for the deposit of silver dollars with the Treasurer of the United States. These certificates were not made legal tender.[11]

The period of the Bland-Allison Act, 1878 to 1890, is sometimes called the period of the "limping standard." The usual requisites of a "limping standard" include: (1) gold freely coined and full legal tender; (2) silver not freely coined; (3) some or all silver coins full legal tender; (4) no legal provision for maintaining the silver monetary unit at par with gold.[12]

Although all of these are descriptive of the Bland-Allison Act, it seems probable that the legal tender quality of the silver coins is not essential to a limping standard. If the silver dollar had not been legal tender at all, or had been limited legal tender to the same extent as the subsidiary silver coins, no appreciable change would have been made in the monetary standard.

Experience under the Bland-Allison Act also illustrates the general principle that legal tender is of secondary importance to convenience in maintaining the acceptability of money. Silver certificates, which were not legal tender, were preferred to the legal tender silver dollars in spite of positive efforts by the government to favor the circulation of the coins. In an effort to create a demand for the coins, the issuance of United States notes in small denominations was discontinued. Treasury disbursing officers paid salaries and current obligations in silver dollars, and offered to place them in people's hands anywhere in the country without cost of transportation. The coins, however, when received, were quickly deposited in local banks, then in city banks, and soon returned to the Sub-Treasuries of the government.[13] By July 1, 1890, silver certificates in circulation outnumbered silver coins almost six to one.

SHERMAN SILVER PURCHASE ACT OF 1890

The Sherman Silver Purchase Act of 1890 authorized the issuance of Treasury notes which were declared to be "a legal tender in payment of all debts, public and private, except where otherwise expressly stated in the contract, and shall be receivable for customs, taxes, and all public dues." These notes were to be used by the Secretary of the Treasury to purchase 4,500,000 ounces of silver each month. The Secretary of the Treasury was directed to redeem the notes on demand in gold or silver coin at his discretion, "it being the established policy of the United

States to maintain the two metals on a parity with each other upon the present legal ratio, or such ratio as may be required by law." No change was made in the legal tender quality of the silver dollars.[14]

The operation of the Sherman Silver Purchase Act provides further evidence that making the standard money legal tender is not sufficient to assure the continued function of the standard as such. No alteration of the legal tender quality of either gold or silver coins was made by the Sherman Act, but its provisions tended to force the adoption of a silver standard by progressively increasing withdrawals of gold from the Treasury.

In an address to a special session of Congress, August 8, 1893, President Grover Cleveland pointed out the difficulties which confronted the country because of the silver purchase requirement. He said:

"Up to the 15th day of July, 1893, these notes [Treasury notes of 1890] had been issued in payment of silver bullion purchases to the amount of $147,000,000. While all but a very small quantity of this bullion remains uncoined and without usefulness to the Treasury, many of the notes given in its purchase have been paid in gold. . . .

"We have thus made the depletion of our gold easy and have tempted other and more appreciative nations to add it to their stock. . . . The excess of gold exports over its imports for the year ending June 30, 1893, amounted to more than $87,500,000.

". . . Unless the Government bonds are to be constantly issued and sold to replenish our exhausted gold, only to be again exhausted, it is apparent that the operation of the silver purchase law now in force leads in the direction of the entire substitution of silver for the gold in the Government Treasury, and that this must be followed by the payment of all Government obligations in depreciated silver."[15]

This tendency toward enforced adoption of a silver standard was not the result of the legal tender quality of the silver dollars, the gold coins, or the Treasury notes. The tendency was changed, not by removing the legal tender quality of the silver dollars, or of the Treasury notes, but by abandoning the silver purchase requirement.

GOLD STANDARD ACT OF 1900

The Act of March 14, 1900, provided for a gold coin standard in the United States by defining the standard unit of value in terms of gold alone, and maintaining the parity of all other moneys with gold by redeeming them, directly or indirectly, in gold. The sections of the Act essential to the adoption of the gold coin standard were:

". . . The dollar consisting of twenty-five and eight-tenths grains of gold, nine-tenths fine . . . shall be the standard unit of value. . . .

". . . All forms of money issued or coined by the United States shall be maintained at a parity of value with this standard, and it shall be the duty of the Secretary of the Treasury to maintain such parity. . . .

". . . United States notes, and Treasury notes . . . when presented to the Treasury for redemption, shall be redeemed in gold coin. . . ."[16]

No change was made in the legal tender qualities of any of the moneys of the United States. The law reaffirmed the legal tender qualities of gold and silver coins—gold coins and silver dollars were full legal tender, and subsidiary silver coins were legal tender up to ten dollars in any one payment.

The provisions of the law essential to establishing a gold coin standard were those providing the definition of the standard unit and the maintenance of parity, including redemption, between the standard unit and other forms of money. The legal tender qualities of gold and silver coins were merely complementary.

B

MONEY RECEIVABLE FOR SPECIFIED PURPOSES

UNITED STATES NOTES

The Act of February 25, 1862, specifically states that United States notes, in addition to being lawful money and legal tender, were "receivable in payment of all taxes, internal duties, excises, debts and demands of every kind due to the United States, except duties on imports, and of all claims and demands against the United States of every kind whatsoever, except for interest on bonds and notes. . . ."[17]

Prior to 1862, money had been designated legal tender *or* receivable for specified purposes, but not both. Legal tender money was received by the Treasury without further legal designation, and other money not made receivable by law was also accepted at times. The quality of being receivable for specified purposes, before 1862, had been confined to money to which Congress did not wish to extend the legal tender quality.

The receivability provision of the United States notes was broader than had been used prior to 1862. The more frequently observed provision referred to receiving the money in payments of all kinds to the government, not to receiving the money in payments by the government.

Both types of receivability clauses are redundant if the money is also full legal tender. The United States notes, although they were not legal tender without exception, had the same exceptions to their use as money receivable for specified purposes. The resulting anomaly can only be explained by a failure of the legislators to understand the significance of the two concepts.[18]

GOLD CERTIFICATES

The Act of March 3, 1863, authorized the Secretary of the Treasury to issue gold certificates on receipt of deposits of gold coin and gold bullion. They were not legal tender, but were to be "received at par in payment for duties on imports," and were redeemable on demand at the Treasury in gold coin or bullion. The Act also authorized the certificates to be used in paying interest on the public debt. At no time were the certificates so issued to exceed 120 percent of the value of the gold coin and bullion then in the Treasury.[19]

The purpose of these certificates appears to have been to provide a convenient means of making the particular payments excepted in the legal tender and receivability provisions of the

United States notes. Parity with gold was maintained by the redemption in gold coin or bullion on demand.

With the resumption of specie payments on January 1, 1879, the issuance of gold certificates was discontinued. By the Act of July 12, 1882, the Secretary of the Treasury was again authorized to issue gold certificates in receipt of deposits of gold coin and gold bullion. These certificates were declared to be "receivable for customs, taxes, and all public dues, and when so received may be reissued."[20] The clause is repeated in the Acts of March 4, 1900, and March 2, 1911.

The gold certificates were receivable in payments to the government until December 24, 1919, when they were made full legal tender.[21]

SILVER CERTIFICATES

Silver certificates issued under the Bland-Allison Act of 1878 were "receivable for customs, taxes and all public dues." The act permitted them to be reissued. A similar provision was made in 1900 for silver certificates issued in exchange for the deposit of silver dollars with the Treasury.[22] The latter issue was designed to replace the Treasury notes of 1890. Silver certificates were not made legal tender until May 12, 1933.

TREASURY NOTES OF 1890

The silver purchase act of July 14, 1890, made the Treasury notes legal tender *and* "receivable for customs, taxes and all public dues." Like the provisions of the law of 1862 authorizing the issue of United States notes, this dual designation was redundant and unnecessary. Being legal tender, they were receivable in payments to the government without special designation in the law. It seems probable that the legislators did not understand the difference between the two concepts.[23]

NATIONAL BANK NOTES

The National Bank Act of 1863,[24] as amended in 1864,[25] authorized banks chartered under the act to issue circulating notes. Section 23 of the act provided that these notes "shall be received in all parts of the United States in payment of taxes, excises, public lands, and all other dues to the United States, except for duties on imports, and also for all salaries and other debts and demands owing by the United States to individuals, corporations and associations within the United States except interest on the public debt and in redemption of the national currency." Section 32 also provided that, "Every association formed or existing under the provisions of this act shall take and receive at par for any liability to the said association any and all notes or bills issued by any association existing under and by virtue of this act."

In several particulars this was a more inclusive receivability clause than had been used up to this time, although similar to the clause in the Act of February 25, 1862, authorizing the issue of United States notes. The bank notes were made receivable in some payments by the government to private individuals, and in some payments by private individuals to the banks. The exceptions of customs payments and interest on the public debt, on the other hand, made the receivability of the national bank notes less inclusive than the Treasury notes and the notes of the First and Second Banks of the United States.

The national bank notes were not legal tender, however. Payments in which they were receivable were confined to transactions to which the government was a party, or in which the government had a special interest, such as payments to the associations organized under the terms and conditions of the act. There was no intention of issuing irredeemable bank paper money. Although Salmon P. Chase, the Secretary of the Treasury, was willing to issue government irredeemable paper money as a temporary expedient, he believed that the bank notes would be payable "after resumption, in specie, on demand; and if not so paid, will be redeemable at the Treasury of the United States from the proceeds of the bonds pledged in security."[26]

The notes apparently were made receivable for the purposes specified in order to avoid the consequences of making them full legal tender. Had they been legal tender, they could have been used in payments between private individuals even if objected to on grounds of their quality, including the discharge of debts contracted prior to the passage of the law. The lawful money provisions for redemption of the notes would have been quite meaningless.[27]

While the government paper money was irredeemable, private creditors received no particular advantage from their right to refuse the national bank notes. The notes were redeemed, in practice, only in the legal tender United States notes. The right to refuse the national bank notes became of more significance after 1879 when the legal tender money of the United States was paid in gold on demand.

FEDERAL RESERVE BANK NOTES

Section 4 of the Federal Reserve Act of December 23, 1913, authorized the issuance of circulating notes by the Federal Reserve Banks, "such notes to be issued under the same provisions of law as relate to the issue of circulating notes of national banks secured by bonds of the United States bearing the circulating privilege. . . ."[28]

The Federal Reserve bank notes thus apparently were made receivable to the same extent as national bank notes, although the words were not repeated in the Federal Reserve Act.

FEDERAL RESERVE NOTES

Section 16 of the Federal Reserve Act also authorized the issuance of Federal Reserve notes "at the discretion of the Federal Reserve Board." These notes were to be "receivable by all national and member banks and Federal Reserve banks and for all taxes, customs, and other public dues."

By making the notes receivable in these payments, the act provided a means of payment. At the same time the legislators avoided any implication of acceptance of them by private individuals, and the full legal consequences of making the notes legal tender. This was in accordance with previous practice with reference to the legal qualities of bank note issues.

Although legal tender and lawful money for reserve purposes are separate and distinct concepts, there has been a tendency in court decisions to make them synonymous. It will be demonstrated that one United States attorney-general contributed significantly to the error. The Reserve Act, however, avoided the paradoxical situation which would have resulted had the courts' erroneous interpretation been followed. If the judicial interpretation of lawful money and legal tender had been adhered to (an impossibility in practice), and if the Reserve Act had made the Federal Reserve notes legal tender, a liability (Federal Reserve notes) could have been interpreted judicially as an asset to be held against another liability (deposits in the Federal Reserve Banks).[29]

The expedient of making the notes receivable in payments to the government and by member banks and Reserve Banks, gave to the notes a legal quality sufficient for the performance of their chief function as media of exchange while retaining both quantitative and qualitative restrictions on their issuance.

C

LAWFUL MONEY

UNITED STATES NOTES

The words "lawful money" first appear in federal statutes in the Act of February 25, 1862, which declared the United States notes to be "lawful money and a legal tender and receivable for the purposes specified."[30] Because this terminology had not appeared before, nor has it appeared since that date, the question arises: Why were both phrases used to describe United States notes in 1862?

Although it is probably impossible to provide absolute proof of the reasons for this terminology in 1862, a logical explanation may be found in the circumstances surrounding the passage of the act.

The words "lawful money" had appeared in many state banking laws from 1837 to 1862.[31] The meaning of lawful money for the reserve purposes specified in these laws was gold and silver. Mr. Elbridge G. Spaulding, who originally introduced the bill authorizing the United States notes into the House of Representatives, was a successful banker of Western New York. It is logical to assume that Spaulding was aware of the meaning of the lawful money provisions of state laws (particularly that of New York), and that the designation "lawful money" in the law of 1862 was intended to make the United States notes legal for use as reserves against the notes and deposits of banks organized under state banking laws.

A definite statement to this effect, so far as this author has been able to ascertain, is not contained in Mr. Spaulding's *History of Legal Tender Paper Money issued during the Great Rebellion*,[32] nor in his speeches in support of the bill in Congress on January 25, 1862,[33] nor in support of a second bill containing a like clause on June 7, 1862.[34]

These speeches by Spaulding, and other members of Congress, were concerned at the time almost exclusively with the effects of the legal tender designation, with the question of the Congress' authority to make them legal tender, and with the exigencies of the war situation with respect to the Treasury. No one seemed concerned about the effect of making the notes lawful money for reserves of banks. It is reasonable to suppose, however, that some reason existed for including the words "lawful money." The banking legislation of the states and the evident desire to give wide acceptance to the United States notes, would seem to provide a reasonable, if inferential, explanation of the wording of the act, since it permitted the notes to serve as reserves against bank deposits.

NATIONAL BANK ACT

The National Bank Act, as amended,[35] created a system of banking associations which could engage in deposit banking and the issuance of circulating notes, and designated the kind of money which could be used as reserves against notes and deposits. The general term for this kind of money was "lawful money."

For the first time, a federal law mentioned the kind of money which could be used as reserves in banks. The First and Second Banks of the United States had overall debt limitations, but no requirement concerning the character of the reserves to be held against such liabilities.

Like the Act of February 25, 1862, the National Bank Act was in part the work of Elbridge G. Spaulding. The use of the words "lawful money" is similar to that of the New York law of 1837, and to some extent of the other state laws as well.

Some national banks were required to keep a legal reserve consisting in part of lawful money, others were required to keep a reserve consisting in part of lawful money and in part of deposits in other banks. Banks were divided into three groups: (1) those located in central reserve cities (only New York until 1887, when Chicago and St. Louis were added); (2) those located in sixteen reserve cities specifically named in the law; and (3) all other national banks. National banks in New York City were required to keep in their vaults a reserve in lawful money of not less than 25 percent of the value of their deposits and notes outstanding. Banks in reserve cities were required to keep a 25 percent legal reserve against deposits and notes outstanding also, but one-half of this amount had to consist of lawful money in their vaults. All other national banks were required to maintain a minimum legal reserve of 15 percent of the value of their notes and deposits, but three-fifths of this amount could consist of deposits with national banks in reserve cities. At least six percent of the value of their deposits and notes outstanding, therefore, had to consist of lawful money in their vaults. No precise definition of lawful money is contained in the act.

The Act of June 20, 1874, removed the requirement of a legal reserve or lawful money reserve to be held against the circulating notes of the national banks.[36] Each bank was required to deposit with the United States Treasury lawful money equal to five percent of its circulating notes, which could be counted as part of its legal reserve against deposits.

The act also provided that national banks could discharge their liability for bank notes outstanding by depositing lawful money to an amount equal in value to the national bank notes. Thereafter the notes would be considered direct liabilities of the Treasury rather than of the issuing bank.

Like the National Bank Act, the Act of 1874 did not define lawful money.

With no definition of lawful money in the statutes, the interpretation of what constituted lawful money within the meaning of the National Bank Act was made by the Comptroller of the Currency and the Treasury authorities. Lawful money, from 1863 to 1882, appears generally to have been interpreted to mean (1) United States notes; (2) gold coin; and (3) silver coin. The national bank legal reserve statement of the Comptroller of the Currency in 1868 includes not only United States notes, gold and silver coins, but also temporary loan certificates of the United States, United States compound interest notes and, of course, due from other banks.[37] Lawful money is not separated from other components of the legal reserve, but the only moneys mentioned are the first three items. Only the United States notes were lawful money by virtue of legislative act—the Act of February 25, 1862, prior to the National Bank Act. The gold and silver coins were never made lawful money except by inference.[38]

Gold and silver certificates were not lawful money, apparently, during the period 1863 to 1882 except for reserves of the national gold banks. They were not designated lawful money in the statutes authorizing their issuance, and they do not appear as part of the legal reserves of national banks in the statements of the Comptroller of the Currency printed in the *Annual Reports of the Secretary of the Treasury* during these years. By the Act of July 12, 1862, gold and silver certificates were made lawful money, by inference, for reserves of the national banks.[39]

The Treasury appears to have considered gold certificates,

gold coins, silver certificates, silver coins, United States notes, Treasury notes of 1890, and subsidiary coins as lawful money for purposes of the redemption funds held by the Treasury against national bank notes and for depositing with the Treasury to discharge a national bank's liability for its national bank notes outstanding.[40]

For the period 1863 to 1913, lawful money seems to have been a broader term than legal tender, including all moneys issued directly by the United States: gold and silver coins which were full legal tender, subsidiary silver and minor coins which were limited legal tender, and gold and silver certificates which were not legal tender. All these were lawful money for one or more of the lawful money purposes in addition to the United States notes, which were specifically labeled lawful money.

THE FEDERAL RESERVE ACT

The words "lawful money" were used in the Federal Reserve Act of December 23, 1913, to describe the kinds of money which could be used legally for several purposes. These purposes included the money to be used (1) by a Federal Reserve Bank to redeem its Federal Reserve notes;[41] (2) by a Federal Reserve Bank to deposit with its Federal Reserve agent and thus reduce its liability for outstanding Federal Reserve notes;[42] (3) by a Federal Reserve Bank as a reserve against its deposits;[43] (4) by a Federal Reserve Bank to reimburse the Treasury for Federal Reserve notes redeemed out of a five percent redemption fund held by the Treasury;[44] (5) to retire and redeem national bank notes;[45] (6) to retire and redeem Federal Reserve bank notes.[46]

The Federal Reserve Act did not specify what moneys were to be considered lawful money for these purposes. Determination of lawful money under the provisions of the act, therefore, was left to the administrative interpretation of the Secretary of the Treasury and the Federal Reserve authorities.

In general, from 1913 to 1933, lawful money for these purposes was interpreted to mean gold, gold certificates, silver dollars, silver certificates, United States notes, and Treasury notes of 1890. Subsidiary silver and minor coins were considered lawful money for some purposes by the Treasury, but not always for reserve purposes by the Federal Reserve authorities. Federal Reserve notes and national bank notes together with Federal Reserve bank notes were not treated as lawful money.[47]

The Treasury acts as the custodian of a reserve in lawful money equal to five percent of the deposits in the Postal Savings Banks. By the Act of June 25, 1910, the Treasurer was required to keep five percent of the deposits in the form of lawful money, but the meaning of lawful money was not otherwise defined. The Act stated:

"Postal Savings funds received . . . shall be deposited in solvent banks . . . but 5 per centum of such funds shall be withdrawn by the board of trustees and kept with the Treasurer of the United States, who shall be treasurer of the board of trustees, in lawful money as a reserve. . . ."[48]

The reserve fund required by the Act of June 25, 1910, apparently is not kept separate from other redemption funds for national bank notes or Federal Reserve bank notes, and apparently is not kept separate from the General Fund of the Treasury. The Daily Treasury Statements, and the Circulation Statement of United States Money issued every six months by the Treasury Department, Bureau of the Public Debt, do not reveal clearly the kinds of money which go to make up these funds. It is evident that the Treasury has often considered money other than gold or gold certificates as lawful money.[49]

STATE BANKING LAWS

The several states have laws regulating the activities of banks organized under their respective authorities. Since 1866, when the federal tax upon the circulation of bank notes issued by state chartered banks became effective, the state banks have not issued circulating notes. Lawful money for purposes of currency redemption funds or reserves against state bank notes have no practical significance in state law. Some states have continued to use the concept of lawful money with respect to reserves to be held by state chartered banks against their deposits, as many did with respect to reserves against bank notes prior to 1863.

While the dual, federal and state, authority governing the operations of banks in the United States continues to exist, the concept of lawful money will continue to be used in state laws, but the state definition of lawful money should be broader than the federal definition because Federal Reserve notes, for example, could be considered good lawful money in non-member state banks.

For example, the State of Delaware requires banks organized under the laws of that state, and subject to its jurisdiction, to maintain a cash reserve of "lawful money of the United States, silver certificates and notes or bills of national banking associations or Federal Reserve notes."[50] Maine requires the cash reserve of its banks to consist of "lawful money of the United States or bank notes of the United States."[51]

There is no logical reason why the lawful money reserves of state banks should not consist of national bank notes, Federal Reserve notes or Federal Reserve bank notes, if such exist. These liabilities of federal banking institutions might be considered proper and desirable assets for state banks to hold as assets against their deposits.

On the other hand, although its does not seem to be the usual practice, there is no reason why state legislatures, or a state banking authority, may not restrict lawful money for reserves against deposits in state banks to silver coin or gold coin (if such coins could be held legally).

No detailed examination of lawful state money reserve requirements against deposits for the period after 1862 is undertaken in this study. Chief emphasis is placed upon Federal laws after that date, and at the present time, because a detailed examination probably would add little to an understanding of the concepts.

FOOTNOTES

[1] 12 *Statutes at Large* 345. The inconsistencies in this law are discussed on pages 106-107.

2 *Cheang-Kee v. United States,* 70 U. S. 320 (1865).
3 *Lane County v. Oregon,* 74 U. S. 229 (1868).
4 *Bronson v. Rodes,* 74 U. S. 229 (1868).
5 Gold certificates are discussed on pages 83-84.
6 The history of the greenback period is a familiar part of American financial history by virtue of Wesley C. Mitchell's studies: *A History of the Greenbacks* (University of Chicago Press, Chicago, 1903) and *Gold, Prices and Wages under the Greenback Standard* (University of California Press, Berkeley, 1908).
7 17 *Statutes at Large* 424.
8 The legal tender quality of the trade dollar was removed by the Act of July 22, 1876, 19 *Statutes at Large* 215, and its coinage suspended by the Act of February 19, 1887, 24 *Statutes at Large* 635. The legal tender quality of silver coins was increased to ten dollars in one payment by the Act of June 9, 1879, 21 *Statutes at Large* 7.
9 20 *Statutes at Large* 25.
10 It seems probable that this clause merely restated the law as it had been interpreted in *Bronson v. Rodes,* 74 U. S. 229 (1868).
11 The legal qualities of these certificates are discussed on page 84.
12 For example, these are the requisites given by Walter E. Spahr in *Economic Principles and Problems* (Farrar and Rinehart, Inc., New York, 1940), 4th ed., Vol. I, p. 447.
13 A more detailed description of the efforts to keep the coins in circulation may be found in Davis R. Dewey, *Financial History of the United States* (Longmans, Green and Co., New York, 1939), 12th ed., pp. 407-408.
14 26 *Statutes at Large* 289.
15 James D. Richardson, ed., *Messages and Papers of the Presidents* (Bureau of National Literature, Inc., New York, 1897), Vol. XII, p. 5835.
16 31 *Statutes at Large* 45.
17 12 *Statutes at Large* 345.
18 The confusion of the concepts in this law is discussed elsewhere.
19 12 *Statutes at Large* 709.
20 22 *Statutes at Large* 162.
21 41 *Statutes at Large* 378.
22 20 *Statutes at Large* 45.
23 26 *Statutes at Large* 289.
24 12 *Statutes at Large* 665.
25 13 *Statutes at Large* 99.
26 *Annual Report of the Secretary of the Treasury on the State of the Finances* (1862), p. 17.
27 The provisions of the act with respect to lawful money are described on pages 89-91.
28 38 *Statutes at Large* 251.
29 This paradox resulted later from the legislation of 1933, which is dis-

cussed on pages 109-111.

[30] 12 *Statutes at Large* 345. The full text of the qualities of these notes is given on page 77.

[31] These laws have been described on pages 68-71.

[32] Express Publishing Company, Buffalo, N. Y., 1869.

[33] *Congressional Globe*, 37th Cong., 2d Sess., p. 525.

[34] *Ibid.*, p. 2767.

[35] 13 *Statutes at Large* 99.

[36] 18 *Statutes at Large* 123.

[37] *Annual Report of the Secretary of the Treasury on the State of the Finances* (1868), p. 8.

[38] The Act of July 12, 1870, specifically states, however, that lawful money, when applied to national gold banks, "shall be held and construed to mean gold and silver coin of the United States."

[39] The actual words "lawful money" were not used. The act made gold and silver certificates eligible for "use as reserves" by national banks.

[40] For example, in the *Annual Report of the Secretary of the Treasury on the State of the Finances* (1891), pp. 10-11; (1893), p. 9.

[41] Sec. 16, par. 1. "Federal reserve notes . . . shall be redeemed in gold on demand at the Treasury Department of the United States . . . or in gold or lawful money at any Federal reserve Bank."

[42] Sec. 16, pars. 5, 6. "Any Federal reserve bank may at any time reduce its liability for outstanding Federal reserve notes by depositing, with the Federal reserve agent, its Federal reserve notes, gold, gold certificates, or lawful money of the United States. . . . The Federal reserve agent shall hold such gold, gold certificates or lawful money available exclusively for exchange for the outstanding Federal reserve notes. . . ."

[43] Sec. 16, par. 3. "Every Federal reserve bank shall maintain reserves in gold or lawful money of not less than thirty-five per centum against its deposits and reserves in gold of not less than forty per centum against its Federal reserve notes in actual circulation, and not offset by gold or lawful money deposited with the Federal reserve agent."

[44] Sec. 16, par. 4. "The Federal Reserve Board shall require each Federal reserve bank to maintain on deposit in the Treasury of the United States a sum in gold sufficient in the judgment of the Secretary of the Treasury for the redemption of the Federal reserve notes issued to such bank. . . ." Sec. 16, par. 3, "Notes presented for redemption at the Treasury of the United States shall be paid out of the redemption fund and returned to the Federal reserve banks through which they were originally issued, and thereupon such Federal reserve bank shall, upon demand of the Secretary of the Treasury, reimburse such redemption fund in lawful money, or, if such Federal reserve notes have been redeemed by the Treasurer in gold or gold certificates, then such funds shall be reimbursed to the extent deemed necessary by the Secretary of the Treasury in gold or gold certificates. . . ."

[45] Sec. 18, par. 1. ". . . Any member bank desiring to retire . . . its

circulating notes, may file with the Treasurer of the United States an application to sell for its account . . . United States bonds securing circulation to be retired." Sec. 18, par. 4. ". . . Each member bank shall duly assign and transfer, in writing, such bonds to the Federal reserve bank purchasing the same, and such Federal reserve bank shall, thereupon, deposit lawful money with the Treasurer of the United States for the purchase price of such bonds. . . ."

46 Sec. 18, par. 6. "[Federal reserve bank notes] . . . shall be in form prescribed by the Secretary of the Treasury, and to the same tenor and effect as national bank notes now provided by law. They shall be issued and redeemed under the same terms and conditions as national bank notes. . . ." By the Act of March 9, 1933, these provisions were changed slightly to read: "Such notes . . . shall be in form prescribed by the Secretary of the Treasury, *shall be receivable at par in all parts of the United States for the same purposes as are national bank notes, and shall be redeemable in lawful money of the United States on presentation at the United States Treasury or at the bank of issue.*"

47 The inconsistencies in Treasury and Federal Reserve interpretation of lawful money are discussed on pages 118-122.

48 36 *Statutes at Large* 816.

49 For example, the *Circulation Statement of United States Money*— December 31, 1946, in a footnote to the total of all other money except that held by the Treasury against gold and silver certificates, United States notes, Treasury notes of 1890, or for the Federal Reserve banks and agents, states: "Includes $164,000,000 lawful money deposited as a reserve for Posal Savings deposits." Because the total in gold includes the Exchange Stabilization Fund of $1,800,000,000 and amounts to $1,942,418,000, a part of the $164,000,000 must consist of money other than gold and gold certificates. No gold certificates are held as "All other money." An unfortunate result of the indefiniteness of these practices is discussed on pages 118-126.

50 *Banking Laws of the State of Delaware* (1936), p. 82.

51 *Revised Statutes of the State of Maine* (1936), Sec. 80.

chapter

6

CONFUSION EXISTING IN THE MEANING, USE, AND SIGNIFICANCE OF THE LEGAL QUALITIES OF MONEY

A
COURT DECISIONS

LEGAL TENDER, LAWFUL MONEY, AND MONEY RECEIVABLE
for specified purposes have not been differentiated clearly by the
courts. Definitions of the terms have been inconsistent, and the
courts have failed to reconcile their opinions either with precedents or with monetary and banking practice and theory. Many
of the decisions must be considered in error.

Court decisions have confused: (1) legal tender and lawful
money in the broad general sense; (2) legal tender and lawful
money in the technical sense; (3) legal tender and money receivable for specified purposes; and (4) lawful money in the
broad sense and lawful money in the technical sense. This confusion is not confined to state court decisions, but occurs as well
in the decisions rendered by the Supreme Court of the United
States.

STATE COURTS BEFORE 1863

The decision in an early case[1] illustrates a confusion of legal
tender and lawful money.

Wharton and Company sold tobacco to Pleasant, Shore and
Company in 1780. Willing, Morris and Inglis, merchants of
Philadelphia, went on bond to assure payment by Pleasant,
Shore and Company in "lawful current money of Pennsylvania"
by September 30, 1782. At the time of the sale, Continental
Currency had been legal tender in Pennsylvania, but the ratio
of depreciation compared to coin was five to one. Subsequently
the Pennsylvania statute making Continental Currency legal
tender had been repealed. When payment was not made at the
appointed time, suit was instigated to collect the amount due.
Plaintiffs argued that, Continental Currency not being legal

tender any longer, they were entitled to collect in gold or silver coin. Defendants argued that "lawful current money" meant what had been current and a legal tender at the time of the sale.

In its decision, the court said:

"What is current lawful money of Pennsylvania? For my part, I know of none that may be so called, for current and lawful are synonymous. In Great Britain, the king, by his proclamation, may render any species of money a lawful currency, while here it is accomplished by act of the legislature. . . . The expression in the Act of the 27th January 1777 cannot be construed to make the Spanish milled dollars a legal tender as they are only mentioned by way of reference; but that which was declared to be a lawful tender, and consequently became the legal currency of the land, was the money emitted under the authority of Congress.

"To that species of money, therefore, the bond must be taken to relate; and the jury will either reduce the penalty to gold or silver, according to the scale of depreciation or, if they think it more equitable, will find a verdict for the tobacco."

Thus, although the court admitted it did not know what lawful money meant, the decision implied that the term meant legal tender. It established a significant but unfortunate precedent.

Although it is not possible to ascertain precisely what the contracting parties meant by the term "lawful current money" or "lawful money," the words appear to have been used popularly to differentiate gold and silver coin from paper bills of credit. The same court, in deciding a suit on a promissory note calling for "current lawful money," refused to admit oral evidence purporting to show that silver coin had been intended by the parties to the contract.[2] Lawful money was used to mean specie or gold and silver coin in state banking laws fifty years later.[3]

A state court in 1833 confused legal tender, lawful money in the broad sense, and money receivable in payments to the state treasury. An indictment, in this case,[4] charged a civil servant with receiving more than the fee allowed him by statute and that this excess had been received in "lawful money of the State of Tennessee." The evidence submitted showed that he had received a state bank note. State bank notes were receivable in payments to the State of Tennessee, and constituted a major part of the media of exchange. They were not legal tender; only gold and silver coins were legal tender in the United States at that time.

The court held that the evidence did not sustain the indictment because "state bank notes are not legal tender and, hence, not lawful money." It appears to be self-evident that the indictment used the words "lawful money" in the broad, general sense. Money in this sense includes all money receivable in specified payments as well as legal tender. The decision contributed nothing to the distinction of these qualities of money.

Similarly, in *Pryor v. The Commonwealth of Kentucky*[5] the court held that lawful money meant "nothing but gold and silver coin," and declined to sustain a charge of keeping a gaming table, where the evidence indicated only that bank notes were bet, lost, and won.

It is not clear whether the court confused lawful money with legal tender because only gold and silver coins were legal tender or because state laws required banks to keep a reserve in lawful money (by which was meant gold and silver coins) against bank notes and deposits. It may have been confused for both reasons.

As an illustration of the inconsistency, other courts at approximately the same time were rendering decisions that lawful money meant any kind of money which circulated from hand to hand, irrespective of the legal tender quality of the money.[6]

STATE COURTS AFTER 1863

Confusion of these qualities in court decisions persisted after the legal tender acts of the Civil War period, and the confusion increased after the passage of the National Bank Act.

In *Parrish v. Kohler,* the court decided that lawful money and legal tender were synonymous terms. Said the court: "At the time of making this mortgage . . . all silver coins were a legal tender for any amount. The stipulation here is for lawful silver money and the contract contemplated nothing more than that five thousand dollars should be paid in silver money then lawful."[7]

An Indiana case in 1877 revealed a confusion of legal tender, lawful money in the broad sense, and lawful money in the technical sense.[8] The court voided an indictment charging larceny of "lawful money of the United States" because no evidence was submitted concerning the character of the money, except that some national bank notes were included. The court said: " 'Lawful money of the United States' might consist of gold and silver coins, or United States Treasury notes and the fractional currency. . . . The notes of the national banks are in no sense lawful money of the United States."

It is not clear, from the decision, whether the court regarded legal tender and lawful money as synonymous. It included in its definition only those kinds of money which were full or limited legal tender. No mention was made of the fact that national bank notes were receivable in most payments to the government, which made them lawful money in the broad sense.[9] The national bank notes were not lawful money in the technical sense, nor were they legal tender. Apparently there was a multiple confusion of the qualities.

A Texas court confused lawful money in the technical sense, lawful money in the broad sense, and legal tender.[10] Citing a long list of precedents, the court said:

"It has been held in a number of decisions that 'lawful money of the United States' means coin or Treasury notes made a legal tender by act of Congress. We are not advised of any case holding that, under our statutes with reference to theft of money, national bank notes or silver certificates are regarded as money."

The court seems to have been of the opinion that lawful money and legal tender were synonymous. Coin and Treasury notes were full or partial legal tender, but national bank notes and silver certificates were receivable in the payments specified by act of Congress. There is no reference here to the fact that silver certificates were lawful money for the purposes of reserves in the national banking system, and redemption funds for national bank notes.

Similarly, an Oregon trial judge was particular to charge

the jury not to find a defendant guilty of embezzling funds unless
they believed the money appropriated was "lawful money of the
United States." The court then said: "The only lawful money
of the United States consists of coins of the United States
and United States Treasury notes, commonly called greenbacks. . . ."[11] Inasmuch as these were the only legal tender
money, the court apparently believed that legal tender and lawful money were equivalent terms.

Several state cases brought forth decisions recognizing the
broad, general meaning of lawful money, but failed to recognize
the difference between lawful money in the broad sense and
lawful money in the technical sense.

An Iowa court in which the defendant was accused of "theft
of lawful money of the United States" cited the cases making
lawful money and legal tender synonymous, but applied a
broader definition.

The court said: "In view of the purposes of the statute, and
the popular understanding of the term 'lawful money of the
United States,' we conclude that the indictment was designed
to include any money which was lawfully circulated in the
United States."[12]

Similarly, in the case of *State v. Finnegan,* the court said:

". . . There are plenty of cases adopting the view that lawful
money does not include bank notes. But they proceed on the
erroneous theory that anything to be money, must be a legal
tender. That bank notes are commonly regarded as money is
not open to debate."[13]

In *Martin v. Bott,*[14] the court stated accurately those kinds
of money which were legal tender at that time, and those which
were lawful money in the technical sense at that time. It failed
to recognize, however, that the quality of being receivable for
specified purposes also applied to national bank notes, gold
certificates, and silver certificates. The court said:

"There is a wide distinction between the terms. . . . A tender,
to be good in law, must be made in the legal tender notes or
coin of the United States. . . . National bank notes and gold and
silver certificates are lawful money but are not legal tender."

A Kansas court in 1921 clearly stated that lawful money

and legal tender were distinct qualities of money. It said nothing, however, about the quality of being receivable for specified purposes. The court said:

"There are numerous statements in judicial opinions which make lawful money the equivalent of legal tender, but the legal tender statute seems to recognize legal tender as a quality additional to lawful money.

"The prevailing conception of lawful money of the United States is money in circulation by sanction of the United States."[15]

The court did not clarify the meaning of the word *sanction*. Sanctioning a money apparently included making the money receivable for specified purposes; national bank notes, therefore, apparently were considered "lawful money." The court criticized severely the decision rendered in *Hamilton v. State*[16] for declaring that "notes of the national banks are in no sense money of the United States."[17]

But national bank notes were not lawful money in the technical sense. They were made redeemable in lawful money by the National Bank Act. It follows, therefore, that the court confused lawful money in the broad and technical meanings.

So far as this author has been able to determine, no case in the state courts has clearly revealed the difference between legal tender, lawful money, and money receivable for specified purposes. The decisions reveal little more than inconsistency and confusion. All the cases having to do with legal tender, lawful money, and money receivable have not been cited, but those cited seem representative of the whole.

THE UNITED STATES SUPREME COURT

Chief Justice Marshall, in *Thorndike v. United States*,[18] clearly stated the law with respect to legal tender, and money receivable for specified purposes, as it was understood at that time (in 1819). Treasury notes issued under the authority of the Act of March 4, 1814,[19] were "receivable in payment of all duties and taxes laid by authority of the United States and of all public lands sold by the said authority." Marshall said these notes "are a good tender and may be pleaded as such to such debts." He further stated that "a tender should always be made in lawful money but, as lawful money is not always legal tender, if objected to other money must be produced."

At this time the technical use of the term "lawful money" was not apparent in either state or federal case law.

The decisions in the Legal Tender Cases do not touch upon the difference between legal tender and lawful money, although the acts authorizing the issuance of United States notes declared them to be "lawful money and a legal tender." The court, in these cases, did not say lawful money meant legal tender; nor did it say they were different concepts. It was concerned solely with the question of whether Congress had the power to authorize such notes.[20]

The Supreme Court was confronted with an ambiguous, puzzling act of Congress which had made the United States notes lawful money, legal tender and receivable in all payments *to* the United States except import duties and interest on the public debt.[21] It did not face the issue squarely. The Court said:

". . . Any construction of the second, or . . . legal tender clause, that includes dues for taxes under the words debts, public and private, must deprive the first clause of all effect whatever."[22]

It seems probable, because of the circumstances surrounding the passage of the Act of February 25, 1862, that the law had been poorly phrased, and the intent of the legislators vaguely and inadequately expressed.[23] But the Court, after admitting the ambiguous nature of the law ruled that "Congress must have had in contemplation debts originating in contract or demands carried into judgement, and only debts of this character."

In *Butler v. Horwitz,* the Supreme Court stated that lawful money meant legal tender. Chief Justice Chase said:

"Damages for non-performance must be assessed in lawful money; that is to say, in money declared to be legal tender in payment, by a law made in pursuance of the Constitution of the United States."[24]

The Supreme Court has never delivered a decision clarifying the meaning of the qualities of money as they have been expressed in federal statutes. Only a combination of consistent court decisions and consistent legislation can remove the confusion which has resulted.

B

FEDERAL LEGISLATION

ACT OF FEBRUARY 25, 1862

The circumstances surrounding the issue of legal tender United States notes in 1862 reveal a lack of understanding, and considerable confusion of thought, on the part of members of Congress concerning the meaning and significance of the concepts of legal tender, lawful money, and money receivable for specified purposes.

Two schools of thought are apparent in the Congress at the time the legislation was being formulated. One was led by Mr. Elbridge G. Spaulding of New York; the other by Mr. Justin Morrill of Vermont. Mr. Spaulding's group favored an issue of Treasury notes which would be full legal tender, on the grounds that this quality was essential to a wide acceptance of the notes, and to secure sufficient revenue for the Treasury. Mr. Morrill's group, although they agreed that an issue of Treasury notes was necessary, were opposed to making them legal tender. The latter group preferred to make the notes receivable in all payments to the Treasury. Mr. Morrill's group argued that making them receivable would permit the notes to be used as money by the public, if it desired to do so; that it was probable that the bills would be so used; that any implication of forcing the public to accept them was unjust and undesirable; and that it was questionable if Congress possessed the power to make the notes legal tender.[25]

No one seems to have pointed out specifically that the two qualities were inconsistent, one with the other.

In the bill which passed the House, the notes possessed both qualities. They were "receivable in payment of all taxes, internal duties, excises, debts, and demands of every kind due to the United States" and "lawful money and a legal tender in payment of all debts, public and private."[26]

When the bill was introduced in the Senate, the Finance Committee, headed by Fessenden, who later became Secretary of the Treasury, amended the bill to except import duties and interest payments on the public debt.[27] The Finance Committee did not seek to amend the bill so as to eliminate the legal tender or lawful money clauses, but this amendment was introduced on the floor of the Senate, and defeated by a vote of 17 to 22.[28]

The bill which became law was thus an anomaly. One part of the law denied what was stated in another, and a major part of the bill was redundant and unnecessary if another part of the law was to have meaning.

Prior to this act, only money which Congress did not wish to make full legal tender had been specifically designated "receivable" in payments to the United States. If the notes were to be receivable in payments to the United States, they should not have been legal tender, as this nullified the purposes and significance of the clause making them receivable. If they were legal tender, there was no need to make them receivable in payments to the United States. Furthermore, the exceptions conflicted both with the legal tender quality of the notes and with the quality of being receivable in payments to the United States. It is reasonable to assume that the notes were made "lawful money" in order that they might serve as reserves under the various state banking laws, but nothing in the act makes this specific.[29]

The Act of February 25, 1862, was hastily conceived, pressure by the Treasury was constant during the debates, and the result indicated considerable confusion of thought on the part of the legislators. In addition to the question of the power of Congress to pass such a law, the courts were confronted with a mass of litigation arising because of the inconsistencies in the law itself.

NATIONAL BANK ACT

The wording of the National Bank Act was loose and poorly

conceived. Reserves to be held by national banks against deposits and notes outstanding were required to consist of "lawful money." But the law permitted things other than money to be counted as part of the legal reserves. The law failed to define white was meant by "lawful money" for the purposes prescribed by the act.

The words "lawful money," "lawful money reserve," and "legal reserve" appear to have been used interchangeably in the act, without careful consideration as to whether the reserve being described is to consist of money, deposits in banks, or evidences of debt of other kinds. The impression is received from reading some of the provisions that the legislators considered a deposit liability as money—an obvious mistake. In other paragraphs it is not clear whether clearing-house certificates are being considered as lawful *money*, or merely assets other than money which could be considered a part of banks' legal reserves.[30]

There seems to be no other conclusion to be reached than that Congress either did not understand or did not express its understanding clearly.

FEDERAL RESERVE ACT

The Federal Reserve Act of December 23, 1913, continued the confusion of the National Bank Act by failing to define the words "lawful money," and compounded the confusion by using the phrases "gold or lawful money" and "gold, gold certificates or lawful money," as though gold and gold certificates were not lawful money.[31]

In fact, gold coin was legal tender and lawful money at all times. Gold and silver certificates were lawful money under the National Bank Act after 1882, and both were receivable in payments to the United States. Gold certificates were not legal tender until 1919, and silver certificates were not legal tender until 1933.

The more accurate and more appropriate wording of the Federal Reserve Act would have been "gold, gold certificates *or other lawful money."*

In 1933 and 1934, Congress injected further confusion into monetary and banking law by legislation which disregarded the history and significance of lawful money, legal tender, and money receivable for specified purposes.

The Thomas Amendment to the Agricultural Adjustment Act of May 12, 1933,[32] as amended by Public Resolution No. 10 of June 5, 1933,[33] made every kind of money issued under the authority of the United States full legal tender. This provision states:

"All coins and currencies of the United States (including Federal Reserve notes and circulating notes of Federal Reserve banks and national banking associations) heretofore or hereafter coined or issued, shall be legal tender for all debts, public and private, public charges, taxes, duties, and dues, except that gold coins, when below the standard weight and limit of tolerance provided by law for the single piece, shall be legal tender only at valuation in proportion to their actual weight."

If the words mean what they say, it thus became possible to pay a debt of any amount with coins of any denomination. This disregards the function of limited legal tender subsidiary coins to prevent expense and annoyance to the payee.

If gold coins are legal tender, as stated in the law, it means that they can be used in any payment within the United States at their face value if not below the standard weight and limit of tolerance. But Section 5 of the Gold Reserve Act of January 30, 1934, states that "all gold coin shall be withdrawn from circulation. . . ."[34]

One law, therefore, denies what is stated in another.

The Gold Reserve Act of 1934 also amended Section 16, paragraph 1, of the Federal Reserve Act as follows:

"Federal Reserve notes . . . shall be redeemed in gold or *lawful money* on demand at the Treasury Department of the United States . . . or in gold or lawful money at any Federal Reserve bank."

The act did not specify what was to be considered lawful money for the purpose of redeeming the Federal Reserve notes.

Inasmuch as all coins and currencies of the United States were legal tender by virtue of the Thomas Amendment and the Public Resolution of June 5, 1933, and inasmuch as the Supreme Court had indicated that it believed legal tender to be the equivalent of lawful money, this provision for redemption of the Federal Reserve notes may be considered meaningless. Even if the decisions of Supreme Court were in error, as seems likely, the Gold Reserve Act's provision for redemption of the Federal Reserve notes is still lacking in clarity.

The Gold Reserve Act also amended Section 16 of the Federal Reserve Act, paragraphs 3, 5, 6, and 8. The original phrases had been "gold or lawful money" and "gold, gold certificates or lawful money." These were amended to read "gold certificates or lawful money." Thus, the confusing implication that gold certificates were not lawful money was continued.

There is some evidence, other than the legislation, which seems to indicate that the members of Congress in 1933 and 1934 did not clearly understand the meaning of the concepts concerning which they were legislating. Apparently some of the members, if not all, did not understand how or why the words "lawful money" had been used in preceding legislation.

On June 3, 1933, for example, the following remarks were exchanged in the Senate concerning the meaning of lawful money with respect to Federal Reserve notes, which are described on their face "redeemable in lawful money on demand":

Mr. LEWIS. "What does my able friend say is the meaning of the words 'lawful money,' if they do not mean such money as the Government has made lawful for the payment of debts?"

Mr. REED. "Of course that is what they mean."

Mr. LEWIS. "Then under this measure it becomes lawful money of the same value as gold."

Mr. REED. "It is lawful money now."

Mr. LEWIS. "The bill [Federal Reserve note] contains a promise that it will be paid in gold or lawful money at any Federal Reserve bank. . . ."[35]

Except in the broad sense of not being illegal, or where used as reserves in non-member banks, Federal Reserve notes had never been lawful money up to this time. Before 1933 they were not legal tender, but were receivable for the purposes specified in the Federal Reserve Act. To make them lawful money, which seems to be what these senators thought was being done at that moment, denies any rational meaning to the provisions in the Federal Reserve Act with respect to lawful money.

On January 23, 1934, during the debate on the Gold Reserve Act of 1934, a similar colloquy in the Senate reveals a lack of understanding of the concept of lawful money:

Mr. LEWIS. "I should like the able Senator to give me his definition of lawful money. The Reserve note is payable in gold or lawful money. What does my able friend say is the meaning of 'lawful money' when it is not gold?"

Mr. FESS. "Any money that is redeemable in gold under the Act of 1900."

Mr. LEWIS. "Does the able Senator feel, when the law says 'gold or lawful money,' that the words are not intended to mean money other than gold?"

Mr. FESS. " . . . We have gold coins, silver coins, subsidiary coins in metals; we also have gold certificates, silver certificates— neither one of which is gold; and in addition we have national bank notes, Federal Reserve notes, Sherman notes of 1890, . . . and Federal Reserve bank notes, which are not gold, but every dollar of which, under the Act of March 14, 1900, is redeemable in gold. That makes them lawful money, and when it is said that they are redeemable in gold or lawful money, it means in gold or money in existence which is redeemable in gold. . . . "[36]

The reasoning exhibited here is an example of almost complete confusion. The congressmen appear to have had no conception of the meaning of lawful money for use as reserves against deposits of banks, or as the concept had been used to define redemption funds for Federal Reserve notes or national bank notes. If anything redeemable in gold were lawful money, and if some of the things redeemable in gold were also redeemable in lawful money, then lawful money is redeemable in itself. If this reasoning were of any value, it would have made a farce of the redemption funds held by the Treasury and the reserves against deposits held by the Federal Reserve banks.

ACT OF JUNE 12, 1945

By the Act of June 12, 1945, Congress removed the words "lawful money" from Section 16, paragraph 3, of the Federal Reserve Act. This section of the Act now reads:

"Every Federal Reserve bank shall maintain reserves in gold certificates of not less than 25 per centum against its deposits and reserves in gold certificates of not less than 25 per centum against its Federal Reserve notes in actual circulation. . . ."[37]

Apparently this was intended to solve the question of whether or not Federal Reserve notes were lawful money in the technical sense, and what constituted lawful money for reserve purposes in the Federal Reserve banks. If it had the more inclusive purpose of solving the question of what constituted lawful money for all the purposes specified in the Federal Reserve Act, it failed. Section 16, paragraphs 1, 5, 6 and 8, still contain the words "gold certificates or lawful money" with respect to the redemption funds held by the Treasury to redeem Federal Reserve notes, and with respect to the methods by which the Federal Reserve banks may reduce their liability for outstanding Federal Reserve notes by depositing "gold certificates or lawful money" with the Federal Reserve agents. The law apparently leaves the question of what shall be considered lawful money for these purposes to the administrative interpretation of the Treasury.

If the legislators had understood the concept of lawful money, a simpler method of amending the law to secure the same ends would have become apparent. For example: "For the purposes specified in this act (or, for the purposes of reserves against deposits in the Federal Reserve banks and reserves against Federal Reserve notes), lawful money shall mean gold certificates."

The Act of June 12, 1945, which remains in effect at the present time, involves a peculiar concept of the meaning and purpose of a reserve. Fundamentally, as is evidenced by the history of reserves, and the use of reserves of all kinds, a reserve is a stock of assets capable of discharging specific liabilities when, and if, necessary. A money reserve has for its purpose the maintenance of a liquid position; a bank's money reserve is to meet the obligations or liabilities of the institution when they come due. Throughout the history of banking in the United States, the basic purpose of providing legal reserves has been to assure liquidity.

Lawful money for reserve purposes, therefore, has been selected because it could be used when circumstances require it. But, as our laws stand at present, the very thing which the law requires as a basic reserve against both the deposits and the notes of the Federal Reserve banks, is the most fixed of all the assets of these banks. Gold certificates cannot be used legally to meet any of the domestic obligations of the Federal Reserve banks at any time although they can be used to meet the demands of foreign central banks. Other kinds of money—silver dollars, silver certificates, United States notes, minor currency—which cannot be used as reserves, are nevertheless the only asset cash which can be paid out. It is illogical and confusing.

C
ADMINISTRATIVE AUTHORITIES

Responsibility for the state of confusion with respect to legal tender, lawful money, and money receivable for specified purposes rests not only with the legislative bodies and the courts but with administrative authorities as well. Administrative bodies have been called upon to exercise quasi-legislative and quasi-judicial functions in administering laws which are themselves ambiguous. But the administrative bodies have contributed to the confusion by inconsistency in the selection and application of principles upon which their actions have been based.

COMPTROLLER OF THE CURRENCY

The reports of the Comptroller of the Currency do not reveal precisely what was considered lawful money for legal reserves of national banks, under the provisions of the National Bank Act.

Lawful money is not separated from other things which could be used as part of the national banks' legal reserves.

The report of the Comptroller of the Currency for the year 1868, for example, contains a legal reserve statement for all national banks. The items listed include United States notes, temporary loan certificates, gold and silver coin, United States compound interest notes, and due from other banks.[38] In the report for 1870, clearing house certificates also appear as part of the legal reserves of national banks.[39]

It may be inferred that the Comptroller of the Currency and the Secretary of the Treasury considered that lawful money meant legal tender, unless otherwise stated in law, although the author has been unable to discover a positive statement to this effect. The legal reserve statements, as printed in the *Annual Reports of the Secretary of the Treasury,* from 1865 to 1882, do not list gold or silver certificates as part of the legal reserves of national banks. These moneys were not legal tender during this period, and had not been designated as lawful money for use in the reserves of the national banks by the Congress, except in the case of the national gold banks, 1870-1884. In 1883, however, after the gold and silver certificates had been made eligible for use as reserves by the national banks, these moneys appear in the legal reserve statements.[40] Moneys which were legal tender during the period 1865 to 1883, whether or not they were specifically designated lawful money, do appear in the legal reserve statements during this period.

The Comptroller of the Currency and the Secretary of the Treasury in 1880 appear to have considered interpreting "lawful money" to mean only United States notes, the only money, up to that time, which had been specifically designated "lawful money." The Attorney General (MacVeagh) was requested to rule upon the meaning of the term "lawful money" under the National Bank Act. MacVeagh stated:

" . . . The term lawful money is understood to apply to every form of money which is endowed by law with the legal tender quality. . . .

"I can come to no other conclusion than that a deposit of lawful money to the amount mentioned in the act will authorize the banking association making the deposit to receive the proportionate amount of its bonds, although the lawful money so deposited be coin instead of legal tender notes."[41]

FEDERAL RESERVE AUTHORITIES

Federal Reserve authorities appear to have had no clear-cut conception of the meaning and significance of lawful money. They have defined lawful money rather consistently as legal tender, but their actions have conflicted, at times, with their own definition. The confusion has persisted from 1914 to the present time, and some of the results have been unfortunate.

In 1915, the Reserve authorities defined lawful money as follows:

" . . . The primary meaning of the term 'lawful money' would seem to be legal tender. Silver certificates and gold certificates, however, have been specifically made available for reserves of national banks. Inasmuch as these reserves have to consist, under the law, of lawful money, it would seem clear that the statutes authorizing such silver and gold certificates for use in reserves would bring them within the meaning of the term 'lawful money of the United States.' "[42]

In 1941, the following question-and-answer exchange was printed in the *Federal Reserve Bulletin*:

"Would it be correct to say that 'lawful money of the United States' as used in Section 16 of the Federal Reserve Act means any currency in denomination of $1 or more?

"Such a statement would not be correct in limiting the amount to $1 or more. While the term 'lawful money' is not defined by law, the decisions of the courts indicate that that term includes the classes of money which are declared by the laws of the United States to be legal tender.

" . . . Accordingly, all coins and currencies of the United States may now be regarded as lawful money. . . . It should be noted that, while Federal Reserve notes are regarded as lawful money, as a matter of practical operation they are not counted as part of a Federal Reserve Bank's reserve against deposits maintained with it."[43]

In 1944, again attempting to answer the question, "What is lawful money?", a spokesman for the Reserve authorities stated: "The term 'lawful money' is not defined by law. However, the decisions of the courts indicate that the term includes those classes of money which are declared by the laws of the United States to be legal tender. . . . "[44]

A further series of questions and answers concerning the meaning of 'lawful money' appears in the same publication, as follows:

"Is this gold [at Fort Knox] 'lawful money'?

" . . . Under the existing laws gold may not circulate as money.

" . . . Would . . . gold certificates be 'lawful money'?

"The gold certificates are lawful money but they are not in general circulation, being held by the Federal Reserve banks as a portion of the legal backing for their note and deposit liabilities.

"Could certificates be issued without reference to gold (or silver), but acceptable by the Government for taxes, that would be 'lawful money'?

"The Constitution gives the Congress power to 'coin money and regulate the value thereof.' Congress has the power to order the issuance of any amount of any type of money, which it may deem 'lawful money.' "[45]

Obviously the Federal Reserve authorities failed to recognize that legal tender, lawful money, and money receivable for specified purposes are different concepts. Although the definitions given consistently maintain that lawful money and legal tender are synonymous, this conflicts with the most rudimentary accounting principles. Moreover, the weakness of this position is revealed by the fact that, in practice, this definition was not followed. In other words, the definition which the Reserve authorities adopted was logically impossible to use in practice.

The weakness of considering legal tender and lawful money as equivalent concepts seems to be recognized by the author of the statement made in 1915. Silver certificates, which were receivable by the Treasury but were not legal tender, were included as lawful money, thus recognizing the inconsistency of court decisions and the fact that silver certificates were lawful money by an act of Congress. After 1933, however, the fact that silver certificates had been made legal tender seems to have made the weakness of their definition less obvious to the Reserve authorities.

The definition of lawful money, as given in the 1941 *Federal Reserve Bulletin,* included Federal Reserve notes and Federal Reserve bank notes because these were legal tender by virtue of the Thomas Amendment, and Public Resolution No. 10, of 1933. But the Reserve authorities *did not* consider these notes as lawful money for reserves against deposits in Federal Reserve banks—and the explanation is not simply "a matter of practical operation."

If the Reserve authorities' definition had been accurate, Federal Reserve notes (and Federal Reserve bank notes, when such existed) would have become lawful money for reserves against deposits in the Federal Reserve banks. A liability of a Federal Reserve bank would have become an asset to be used as a reserve against another liability of the bank. Furthermore, since Federal Reserve notes and Federal Reserve bank notes are redeemable, according to law, in lawful money, the notes would have become redeemable in themselves, and the provisions of law with respect to redemption would become meaningless.

There are other actions by the Federal Reserve authorities which conflict with their stated definition of lawful money.

The first report of the Federal Reserve Board, for example, includes national bank notes in the statement of reserves against deposits in the Reserve banks.[46] There is nothing in the Federal Reserve Act to indicate that national bank notes were or were not to be considered lawful money as reserves against deposits. National bank notes were not legal tender, but were receivable for purposes specified in the National Bank Act. They were not lawful money under the National Bank Act, for this would have made an asset out of a liability of the national banks, and the provision for redemption of the notes in lawful money would have been meaningless. This action by the Reserve authorities was in direct conflict with their own definition.

A different conflict is apparent in another practice of the

Reserve authorities. Prior to 1933, Federal Reserve banks carried subsidiary silver coins and minor coins as "non-reserve" cash. These coins were limited legal tender, and were liabilities of the Treasury, not the Reserve banks. Yet they were not considered lawful money for reserve purposes by the Reserve authorities.[47]

There was no logical reason for excluding these coins from the reserves. The fact that the coins were limited legal tender at that time is of no importance, inasmuch as silver certificates were included although they were not legal tender at all.

FEDERAL RESERVE AUTHORITIES AND THE TREASURY

The Treasury and the Federal Reserve authorities have substituted, at times, a deposit credit for purposes which, according to law, required the use of lawful money. They appear to have confused lawful money and a deposit credit—obviously entirely different things.

The Federal Reserve Act provided for a deposit of lawful money in the process of retiring Federal Reserve bank notes and national bank notes. Federal Reserve banks, after purchasing bonds having the circulation privilege, and before receiving Federal Reserve bank notes from the Comptroller of the Currency, were required to "deposit lawful money with the Treasurer of the United States for the purchase price of such bonds."[48] With respect to Federal Reserve bank notes, Section 18, paragraph 6 states: "They shall be issued and redeemed under the same terms and conditions as national bank notes." The National Bank Act had provided that a national bank "may, upon the deposit of lawful money with the Treasurer of the United States ... take up the bonds which said association has on deposit with the Treasurer for the security of such circulating notes. . . ."[49]

If the English language means anything, the National Bank Act and the Federal Reserve Act contemplated the establishment of separate funds, consisting of a specific amount of a particular kind of money (lawful money) of which the Treasurer of the

United States would be custodian. This is evident, not only from the provisions of Section 18 of the Reserve Act, but from the provisions of other sections as well. Section 16, paragraph 3, for example, states: "Notes presented for redemption *at the Treasury of the United States* shall be paid out of the redemption fund and returned to the Federal reserve banks through which they were originally issued, and thereupon such Federal reserve bank shall, upon demand of the Secretary of the Treasury, reimburse such redemption fund in lawful money. . . ."[50] Section 15, paragraph 1, states: "The moneys held in the general fund of the Treasury, *except the five per centum fund for the redemption of outstanding national bank notes and the funds provided in this Act for the redemption of Federal reserve notes may,* upon the direction of the Secretary of the Treasury, be deposited in Federal reserve banks, which banks, when required by the Secretary of the Treasury, shall act as fiscal agents of the United States. . . ."[51]

The Act of March 9, 1933, amended Section 18, paragraph 6, of the Federal Reserve Act by striking out the words, "They shall be issued and redeemed under the same terms and conditions as national bank notes," and adding, "The Secretary of the Treasury is authorized and empowered to prescribe regulations governing the issuance, redemption, replacement, retirement and destruction of such circulating notes and the release and substitution of security therefor. . . ."[52]

The Act of March 9, 1933, did not amend Section 18, paragraph 4; Section 16, paragraph 3; Section 15, paragraph 1; or Section 4, paragraph 4, which states: " . . . such notes [Federal Reserve bank notes] to be issued under the same conditions and provisions of law as relate to the issue of circulating notes of national banks secured by bonds of the United States bearing the circulation privilege. . . ." The Treasury and the Federal Reserve authorities appear to have acted as if these provisions of law had also been repealed.

The method provided for issuing and retiring Federal Reserve bank notes seems clear: First, the Federal Reserve bank applying for the notes to the Treasurer of the United States, was to deposit bonds or other paper specified to the amount of the notes;[53] second, the Reserve bank would deposit with the Treasurer lawful money equal to five percent of the notes placed in circulation, thus reducing the bank's lawful money reserve against its deposits; third, the Treasury would collect a tax of one-fourth of one percent each half year on the average amount of the notes in circulation—the tax thus acting as a continuous pressure to retire the notes; fourth, in order to release the bonds deposited and to retire the notes, the Federal Reserve bank would deposit lawful money with the Treasurer for the amount of the issue; fifth, as the notes were received by a Reserve bank, they would be sent to the Treasury for cancellation, and the issuing bank would receive, in turn, its lawful money.

The Treasury and the Federal Reserve banks did not adhere to the procedure set forth in the Federal Reserve Act. For the purposes of retiring Federal Reserve bank notes, national bank notes, and for reimbursing the redemption funds of the Treasury against Federal Reserve notes and Federal Reserve bank notes, the Federal Reserve notes transferred credit on their books to the general fund of the Treasury.[54] Apparently this was done pursuant to a regulation issued March 31, 1933, by Acting Secretary of the Treasury Ballantine, which permitted Federal Reserve banks to obtain credit in the redemption fund of the Treasury, and to retire Federal Reserve bank notes "by credits in the Treasurer's general account."[55]

One consequence of this misinterpretation of lawful money showed up clearly in the issuance of $660,000,000 of Federal Reserve bank notes during 1942 and 1943. In effect, it amounted to an issue of unsecured paper money in a manner which obscured its nature.[56]

From December 12, 1942, to 1944, the Treasury and the Federal Reserve banks placed in circulation Federal Reserve bank notes in a manner quite different from that prescribed in law. The Treasury deposited unissued notes with the Federal Reserve banks, and received a deposit credit in the general account of the Treasury. This deposit credit, the Reserve authorities insisted, constituted a deposit of lawful money.[57]

The deposit credit received by the Treasury could be spent in exactly the same manner as any other deposit credit obtained through tax receipts or the sale of government obligations. The Reserve banks paid out the notes received from the Treasury, and the Treasury spent the credit. Liabilities of the Treasury were increased, inasmuch as the Treasury assumed the liability of the notes, *but both the deposit credit on the books of the Reserve banks and the bank notes were in use at the same time.* The total amount of money, therefore, was increased by $660,-000,000 (the amount of the issue) more than it would have been had the notes been issued according to the law. In addition, these notes served as lawful money for reserves in the Federal Reserve banks. At the legal ratios then existing, these notes, as lawful money, could support many times their value in deposits of the Federal Reserve System.

It is obvious that a deposit credit on the books of the Reserve banks is not lawful money. The law did not contemplate issuing and redeeming these notes in this manner.[58] The Reserve authorities and the Treasury failed to obey the letter and spirit of the law.

Although the Federal Reserve authorities stated that lawful money meant legal tender, and that a deposit credit with the Reserve banks was lawful money, they acted as if they believed lawful money to be the equivalent of Treasury currency. This is illustrated by the fact that silver certificates were included as lawful money when they were not legal tender, and by the fact that the Federal Reserve bank notes issued in the years 1942 and 1943 as liabilities of the Treasury, were considered by the Federal Reserve banks as "reserves other than gold."

Inconsistent with this interpretation of lawful money, on the other hand, is the treatment of subsidiary silver and minor coin as "non-reserve cash" prior to 1933, and the inclusion in 1915 of national bank notes as reserves, and therefore lawful money.

It is more defensible for the Federal Reserve authorities to consider Treasury currency as lawful money than to consider legal tender as lawful money. The question of lawful money for bank reserves is a question of what are to be considered proper cash assets to be held against certain liabilities. There is no reason, therefore, why moneys which are liabilities of the Treasury should not be considered lawful money for reserves against deposits in the Reserve banks whether or not they are legal tender. On the other hand, there is every reason why moneys which, although legal tender, are liabilities of the Reserve banks, cannot serve as assets of the same institutions.

If the provisions of the Federal Reserve Act are observed, it is impossible for the Federal Reserve notes of one Federal Reserve bank to be considered lawful money for reserves against deposits in another Federal Reserve bank. Section 16, paragraph 3, states: "Whenever Federal reserve notes issued through one Federal reserve bank shall be received by another Federal reserve bank, they shall be promptly returned for credit or redemption to the Federal reserve bank through which they were originally issued or, upon direction of such Federal reserve bank, they shall be forwarded direct to the Treasurer of the United States to be returned. No Federal reserve bank shall pay out notes issued through another. . . . "

Even without the provision quoted above, which was superseded in 1955, it would be improper for one Federal Reserve bank to consider the Federal Reserve notes of another Reserve bank as lawful money against deposits. A liability of one branch of the same basic institution cannot serve logically as an asset of another branch. Furthermore, to make the Federal Reserve notes of one branch lawful money for reserves against deposits in another would render any quantitative requirement for reserves against deposits in the system of somewhat dubious value.

There is, of course, no reason why Federal Reserve notes should not be considered lawful money for reserves against deposits in non-member state banks.[59]

THE TREASURY

The following exchange of letters, reprinted in *American Affairs*[60] with the caption, "A Dollar is a Dollar is a Dollar," reveals considerable confusion of thought concerning the concept of lawful money on the part of some Treasury officials:

December 9, 1947

Honorable John W. Snyder
Secretary of the Treasury
Washington, D. C.

Dear Sir:

I am sending you herewith via Registered Mail one ten-dollar Federal Reserve note. On this note is inscribed the following:

"This note is legal tender for all debts, public and private, and is redeemable in lawful money at the United State Treasury or at any Federal Reserve Bank."

In accordance with this statement, will you send to me $10.00 in lawful money.

Very truly yours,
A. F. DAVIS

encl.
Registered Mail
Return Receipt Requested

TREASURY DEPARTMENT
FISCAL SERVICE
WASHINGTON, 25

Office of Treasury of the United States
In replying please quote JLS:mw

December 11, 1947

Mr. A. F. Davis
12818 Colt Road
Cleveland 1, Ohio

Dear Mr. Davis:

Receipt is acknowledged of your letter of December 9th with enclosure of one ten-dollar ($10.) Federal Reserve Note.

In compliance with your request, two five-dollar United States notes are transmitted herewith.

Very truly yours,
(a) M. E. SLINDEE
Acting Treasurer

Enclosures.

December 23, 1947

Mr. M. E. Slindee
Acting Treasurer
Treasury Department
Fiscal Service
Washington 25, D. C.

Dear Sir:

Receipt is hereby acknowledged of two $5.00 United States notes, which we interpret from your letter are to be considered as lawful money. Are we to infer from this that the Federal Reserve notes are not lawful money?

I am enclosing one of the $5.00 notes which you sent to me. I note that it states on the face:

"The United States of America will pay to the bearer on demand five dollars."

I am hereby demanding five dollars.

Very truly yours,
A. F. DAVIS

AFDavis: NW
Enclosure
Registered Mail
Return Receipt Requested

TREASURY DEPARTMENT

TREASURY DEPARTMENT
FISCAL SERVICE
WASHINGTON, 25

Office of Treasurer of the
United States

December 28, 1947

In Replying Please Quote JLS:mw
Mr. A. F. Davis
12818 Colt Road
Cleveland 1, Ohio

Dear Mr. Davis:

Receipt is acknowledged of your letter of December 23d, transmitting one $5. United States note with a demand for payment of five dollars.

You are advised that the term "lawful money" has not been defined in federal legislation. It first came into use prior to 1933 when some United States currency was not legal tender but could be held by national banking associations as lawful money reserves. Since the act of May 12, 1933, as amended by the Joint Resolution of June 5, 1933, makes all coins and currency of the United States legal tender and the Joint Resolution of August 27, 1935, provides for the exchange of United States coin or currency for other types of such coin or currency, the term "lawful currency" no longer has special significance.

The $5. United States note received with your letter of December 23d is returned herewith.

Very truly yours,
(s) M. E. SLINDEE
Acting Treasurer

Enclosure.

These letters do more than reveal confusion of thought on

the part of Treasury officials. They testify, eloquently and unequivocally, to the fact that the present monetary and banking structure of the United States is saturated with inconsistencies.

If the concepts of legal tender, lawful money, and money receivable for specified purposes are to have meaning, as their nature demands, if they are to serve their necessary and proper functions, the poorly worded monetary laws should be altered, in the interests of consistency, in order to permit these basic concepts to perform their appropriate roles.

FOOTNOTES

1 *Wharton et al. v. Morris et al.,* 1 Dall. 124 (1785). Gouverneur Morris argued the case for the defendants.

2 *Lee v. Biddis,* 1 Dall. 170 (1786).

3 These laws are discussed on pages 68-71.

4 *Garner v. State,* 13 Tenn. 160 (1833).

5 2 Dana (Ky.) 298 (1836).

6 *M'Eowen v. Rose,* 5 N.J. Law 582 (1819); *Griffin et al. v. Thompson,* 43 U.S. 244 (1844).

7 11 Phila. (Pa.) 346 (1876).

8 *Hamilton v. State,* 60 Ind. 193 (1877).

9 Treasury notes receivable in all payments to the United States were called lawful money (in the broad sense) by the Supreme Court decision in *Thorndike v. U.S.,* 2 Mason 1 (1819).

10 *Perry v. State,* 42 Tex. Cr. R. 540; 61 S.W. (Tex.) 400 (1901).

11 *State v. Neilon,* 43 Ore. 168; 73 Pac. (Ore.) 321 (1903).

12 *State v. Boomer,* 103 Iowa 106; 72 N.W. (Iowa) 424 (1897).

13 127 Iowa 286 (1905).

14 46 N. E. (Ind.) 151 (1897).

15 *State v. Elliott,* 202 Pac. (Kan.) 847 (1921).

16 60 Ind. 193 (1877).

17 The judge modified his criticism somewhat by pointing out that the decision in *Hamilton v. State* "was rendered in 1877, before paper currency came to par, and when much confusion of thought respecting the subject of money prevailed."

18 2 Mason 1 (1819).

19 3 *Statutes at Large* 100.

20 *Hepburn v. Griswold,* 8 Wall. 603 (1869); *Knox v. Lee; Parker v. Davis;* 12 Wall. 457 (1870); *Juilliard v. Greenman,* 110 U.S. 421 (1884).

21 The precise wording is given on page 77.

[22] *Lane County v. Oregon,* 7 Wall. 71 (1868).

[23] The ambiguity of the law is discussed on pages 106-107.

[24] 7 Wall. 258 (1868); italics supplied. This decision was cited by the Attorney General in support of his opinion that lawful money meant legal tender in 18 *Opinions of the Attorneys General 121* (1881).

[25] *Congressional Globe,* 37th Cong. 2d Sess. (February 4-5, 1862), pp. 524-635.

[26] *Ibid.* (February 6, 1862), pp. 693-695.

[27] *Ibid.* (February 12, 1862), pp. 763-767.

[28] *Ibid.* (February 13, 1862), pp. 791-795.

[29] The reasons for this inference are given on pages 87-88.

[30] 13 *Statutes at Large* 99. The looseness of the provisions with reference to lawful money is evident in paragraphs 304, 313, 314, 315, 403, 415, 417, 703, 710, 711, 714.

[31] 38 *Statutes at Large* 251.

[32] 48 *Statutes at Large* 51.

[33] 48 *Statutes at Large* 112.

[34] 48 *Statutes at Large* 337.

[35] *Congressional Record,* Vol. 77, p. 4923.

[36] *Congressional Record,* Vol. 78, p. 1136.

[37] 59 *Statutes at Large* 237.

[38] *Report of the Secretary of the Treasury on the State of the Finances* (1868), p. 8.

[39] *Report of the Secretary of the Treasury on the State of the Finances* (1870), pp. 34-35.

[40] *Report of the Secretary of the Treasury on the State of the Finances* (1883), p. 13.

[41] 17 *Opinions of the Attorneys General 118* (1881). This had the unfortunate result of contributing to the fiction that lawful money meant legal tender.

[42] *Federal Reserve Bulletin* (1915), Vol. 1, p. 12.

[43] *Federal Reserve Bulletin* (1941), Vol. 27, p. 630.

[44] *Federal Reserve Bulletin* (1944), Vol. 30, p. 234.

[45] *Ibid.,* p. 235.

[46] *Annual Report of the Federal Reserve Board* (1914), p. 202.

[47] Examples may be found in *Federal Reserve Bulletin* (1923), Vol. 9, pp. 145, 538; *Annual Report of the Federal Reserve Board* (1932), p. 58.

[48] 38 *Statutes at Large* 251, Section 18, paragraph 4.

[49] 31 *United States Code Annotated* 124.

[50] Italics supplied.

[51] Italics supplied.

[52] 48 *Statutes at Large* 1.

[53] However, if the deposit consisted of other than direct obligations of the United States, the bank could receive circulating notes equal to only 90 percent of the face value of the securities deposited.

54 *Annual Report of the Board of Governors of the Federal Reserve System* (1935), pp. 27-28; *Federal Reserve Bulletin* (1935), Vol. 19, pp. 203, 496-497.

55 *Hearings before the Senate Committee on Banking and Currency* (February 17, 1943), 78th Cong., 1st Sess., p. 28.

56 This transaction is described in detail in Walter E. Spahr, *The Manipulation of Our Federal Reserve Bank Notes* (Econimists' National Committee on Monetary Policy, New York, 1944). It is also discussed by William H. Steiner, in "The Federal Reserve Bank Note: Some Observations on Bank Note Issue and Retirement," *Money and the Law* (New York University School of Law, New York, 1945), pp. 73-82.

57 The memorandum presented to the Senate Committee on Banking and Currency by E. A. Goldenweiser of the staff of the Board of Governors stated that ". . . lawful money was deposited with the Treasurer of the United States by giving the Treasurer a deposit account at the Federal Reserve banks. . . ." *Hearings . . . loc. cit.*, p. 29.

58 Professor Spahr, *op. cit.*, p. 12, has pointed out that the Reserve authorities took the position that the Federal Reserve bank notes were "retired" before they were issued—a peculiar interpretation of the meaning of the word *retire*.

59 They are considered lawful money for this purpose in some states. This question is discussed on pages 92-93.

60 (April, 1948), Vol. X, No. 2, p. 88.

chapter

7

PRINCIPLES AND INTERRELATIONSHIPS OF THE LEGAL QUALITIES OF MONEY

A

THE LEGAL QUALITIES OF MONEY
AND THE FUNCTIONS OF MONEY

PURPOSE OF DIFFERING LEGAL QUALITIES

THE FUNDAMENTAL PURPOSE IN DISTINGUISHING DIFFERENT legal qualities of money is to classify various kinds of money in accordance with their legal and economic functions. This is not to deny that designating legal qualities of money may be used for ulterior economic and political purposes. This is not, however, the fundamental purpose.

It appears to be generally agreed that money and monetary problems arose first without governmental activity; that, for the most part, money appeared naturally in the evolution of economic societies probably as the result of voluntary decisions of those engaged in commerce. Law merely stepped in to give sanction to practices after they had been accepted by the community.[1] In a primitive society, therefore, with exchange only a step or two removed from barter, monetary functions were simple enough to obviate the use of different legal qualities of money. As credit instruments became more numerous and more complex, as money and credit came to perform more and different functions, different legal qualities of money came into use. It is probable that the use of more than one legal quality of money is confined to highly specialized credit economies.

FUNCTIONS OF MONEY

The majority of monetary textbooks recognize at least four or five distinct functions of money in modern economic societies.[2] These include the function of a standard of value, or common denominator of value, which facilitates comparison of the relative values of goods at a given time. It also functions as a standard of deferred payments, which facilitates continuity in the statement of value over time; that is, so that obligations having a significant time element may be expressed in terms of a monetary unit capable of comparing values at the time a contract is made and at the time of maturity and payment. A third function is to serve as a means of storing value over time, thus separating the two parts of the transfer process — receiving and spending. In addition to these, money serves as a medium of exchange, and of payment, and as a means of providing reserves against bank deposits and bank notes.

It is unnecessary to elaborate further upon these functions. The works already cited above provide more extended discussion.[3] But for the purposes of this study, it is desirable to divide these functions into two groups: (1) those which relate to the *standard* of measurement of value; and (2) those which relate to the means or media of such measurement.

MONETARY STANDARDS AND LEGAL QUALITIES OF MONEY

Developing a monetary system requires a monetary standard which, in turn, involves selecting a monetary unit, its multiples and fractional parts (such as a dollar or peso), and determining the size and material of which the monetary unit shall be composed. This is exactly analogous to the selection and definition of units of measurement in all sciences. It would, in fact, be impossible to develop a science without there being means of expressing quantitative relations among the phenomena observed. We have thousands of such standards to measure force, weight, distance, mass, and many more. After the development of many of these units, more precise definition is often undertaken by law in the interests of universality and protection of the standard unit by examining the means of its use.

Money, too, requires a standard unit and the two functions mentioned first above, standards of value and of deferred payments, involve the definition of a standard monetary unit. The latter three functions of money involve means or media of measuring value. They bear a relation to the standard monetary unit similar to that which a yardstick or a tape measure bears to a yard. It is no more necessary to measure value exclusively in terms of standard money than it is to measure length exclusively in terms of the standard unit of length. There can be no doubt that measurement, whether of value, length, area, volume, force, or other attribute, will be more accurate if the standard unit is *also the means* by which the measurement is accomplished. Necessity, convenience, or economy may warrant the use of substitutes for the standard unit.

A simple analogy may make this relation clear. The meter, basic unit of the metric system of measuring length and area, is defined as the length of a certain "platinum-iridium bar when supported in a definitely specified manner, at the temperature of melting ice, and at standard atmospheric pressure. . . ."[4] Obviously, a meter is seldom measured by such a bar directly, but it often is measured by a piece of wood, or steel, or cloth, or even plastic, which more or less imperfectly represents it.

The relationship of certain forms of money to the standard money is similar to the relationship of the steel, cloth, or plastic to the meter of platinum-iridium. Logically, the material of which the standard money is composed is selected because it possesses certain characteristics or qualities which make it a good *standard* for the measurement of value and deferred payments. The qualities of acceptability, cognizability, durability, scarcity, divisibility, uniformity, convenience, malleability are often mentioned as desirable qualities for standard money. These same characteristics may be, and ordinarily are, also desirable in the means of measuring value. But there is no logical necessity for this to be so and some of the qualities may be much more significant for the standard money than for money representing the standard.

Since the selection of the standard money does not mean, *ipso facto,* the enforcement of its use in measuring value, some of the other units or types of money may be considered appropriate for some measurements and not others—for some monetary functions and not others.[5] In the United States, the legal qualities of legal tender, lawful money, and money receivable for specified purposes have been used in law to designate moneys which may be used in particular value measurements. The terms have been used for other purposes as well, but this appears to be the most enduring and significant one.

B
LEGAL TENDER

The phrase "legal tender," or its equivalent, appears as a part of all law from which American law stems; that is, it appears in Roman law, English law, and French law. In its fundamental sense, it is an offer to pay a debt, or to settle damages from a trespass or slander, or other act. Under the Code Napoleon, Title III, s. 1258, for example, it is specified that a legal tender, or valid offer of payment, must be made through a ministerial officer. Thus, in every action of debt, covenant, trespass, trover, slander or libel it is possible to make and to plead a tender, or to bring the money due into court.[6]

In highly developed credit economies, in order to avert uncertainties resulting from interpretations of contracts, and to specify the nature of the money to be paid where specific performance is not possible, the phrase "legal tender" means that kind of money which can be validly offered in payment of a debt. In the United States money which has been designated legal tender, without exception, by appropriate authority may be used to measure value in any payment or transaction involving money within the jurisdiction of that authority. These include: (1) payments arising out of breach of contract, or damages for an injury sustained; (2) payments involving a debtor-creditor relation; (3) payments involving a buyer-seller relation; (4) payments by a subject to his government; and (5) payments by a government to its subjects.

— 134 —

LEGAL TENDER AND THE MONETARY STANDARD

There appears to have been a tendency, by the writers of textbooks in money and banking, to describe legal tender as a necessary quality of standard money, to make legal tender a necessary quality of standard money.[7] Although the standard money usually has been legal tender and most difficulties have occurred when non-standard money is made legal tender, both logic and experience indicate that the legal tender quality is not inherent in standard money, and that making standard money legal tender can have meaning only if the standard money circulates domestically.

The evolution of money clearly indicates that things can be widely used and accepted as means of payment without being legal tender.[8] Gold and silver, described by weight and fineness, for example, seem to have been used in Mediterranean trading centers without any seal of authority of a ruler or government, without any super authority to enforce contracts, and before the concept of legal tender was recognized.[9] The evidence indicates that a standard for measuring value originated in the voluntary efforts of merchants to achieve convenience and certainty in the performance of contracts, and that this preceded both the designation of legal tender and the enforcement of contracts by governments.[10]

Subsequently governments established legal monetary standards, coined money, and sometimes issued promises to pay the money they had previously coined or defined. In time also, governments designated their coins or even their promises to pay legal tender and recognized such money as usable in payments between private parties and the government and between two or more private parties.

It should be emphasized that the two acts (1) of coining and (2) of designating legal tender, although complementary, are not identical, and the selection of a standard money is also a separate action, although logically related to coining and to legal tender.

That defining the standard money and designating legal tender are separate acts is clearly illustrated by the division of powers under the Articles of Confederation. Congress had the "sole and exclusive right and power of regulating the value and alloy of coin struck by their own authority, or by that of the respective states. . . ."[11] But the states retained their power to designate coins or paper money bills of credit legal tender; they designated their own paper money legal tender, and the promises issued by the Continental Congress as well. It seems evident that the states had the power to designate legal tender, but the Continental Congress had the power to determine the standard money.[12]

England provides a further illustration. From May 1925 to September 1931, gold was the standard money of England but was not legal tender. Gold was not coined, and the Bank of England was not required to redeem its notes on demand. Instead the Bank was required to buy and to sell gold bars of not less than 400 ounces at the statutory price of gold.[13]

The British were quite logical in this period, for under such a standard (usually called a gold bullion standard), to describe gold as legal tender would be both confusing and misleading. Gold, as legal tender, implies that it can be used in payments of all kinds when, in fact, gold under a gold bullion standard is not circulating money at all but a special commodity in terms of which the unit of account is defined.[14]

HISTORICAL RELATION OF LEGAL TENDER AND STANDARD MONEY

Although standard money is not necessarily legal tender, there has customarily been a close relation between the two, and the standard money is more often legal tender than not. Very often the legislative act, or proclamation, which defined the standard monetary unit also designated a coin or currency composed of or representing that unit (or some multiple thereof) as legal tender. When there is only one kind of money, and that is standard money, the necessity of separating the act of coining or issuing from the act of designating legal tender is obviated. However, if different things circulate from hand to hand as money, the specific designation of some kind or kinds as legal tender may become a necessity for convenience, to protect a worthy debtor or creditor and to prevent or end litigation.

In Roman law, for example, citizens both of the Republic and the Empire were compelled to accept whatever money the government coined. This applied to all payments—to those between private persons as well as between the government and private persons. No explicit designation of legal tender was made. The enforcing acceptance of a money was not separated from the power to coin money.[15]

In England, too, prior to the eighteenth century, coins seem to have been made legal tender implicitly by royal proclamations and the mint indentures which accompanied acts of the Crown in coining money. It should be remembered that money consisted of coin and nothing else and therefore no differentiation of the legal qualities of various kinds of money was necessary.[16]

When several kinds of money, including promises to pay, came to be used simultaneously there occurred explicit designation of legal qualities of money. This was essential to smooth out the uncertainties in otherwise determining which of several kinds of money had the highest recognition, and which kind or kinds could be used in what payments.

An early example of how several different legal qualities of money came to be recognized is illustrated by the attempt of Henry III to introduce gold into the English coinage system in 1257. Although England had used silver coins almost exclusively prior to that time, Henry proceeded to coin a penny of fine gold and to proclaim the rates at which it would "pass current" in terms of the various silver coins then in circulation. His action, in effect, established a rudimentary bimetallic standard with equal recognition of the two metals at the relative rates specified by Henry. The single coinage act by the king involved both selection of the monetary standard and the designation of legal tender as the concept was understood at the time.[17]

For reasons which are not pertinent here, Britons objected to the gold coins. In other words they objected to the King's giving equal recognition to both silver and gold coins—at least at the rates specified in the royal proclamation. Henry subsequently proclaimed that none of his subjects should be required to accept the gold coins, although the King would continue to accept them at the rates indicated in the previous proclamation. This had the effect of removing the legal tender quality of the gold coins. Henry also provided for the exchange of gold and silver pennies, penny for penny, at the royal mint, and stopped minting the gold coins.[18] This restored, in effect, a silver monometallic standard, but the redemption feature so protected the gold coins that some continued to circulate.[19]

Legislation which provided the basis for a gold coin standard in England in 1816[20] also altered the legal tender qualities of gold and silver coins. The wording of the act reveals that the members of Parliament considered the quality of unlimited legal tender to be an important and desirable, if not necessary, quality of the standard money. The pertinent section of the act reads:

> "And whereas at various times heretofore the coins of this realm of gold and silver have been equally a legal tender for payments to any amount, and great inconvenience has arisen from both those precious metals being concurrently the standard measure of value and equivalent for property; and it is expedient that the gold coin made according to the indentures of the mint should henceforth be the sole standard of value and legal tender for payment, without limitation of amount, and that the silver coin should be a legal tender for a limited amount only, for the facility of exchange and commerce:
>
> "Be it therefore enacted, that from and after the passing of this act, the gold coin of this realm shall be considered and is hereby declared to be the only legal tender for payments except as hereinafter provided . . . and no tender of payment of money made in silver coin of this realm of any sum exceeding the sum of forty shillings at any one time, shall be reputed a tender in law. . . ."[21]

The same act limited the coinage of silver and reduced its price in terms of gold. Prior to 1816, silver had been freely coined at a price of sixty-four shillings per ounce, which now was reduced to sixty-two shillings. The actual effect of the limited legal tender provision for silver coins, therefore, was to provide a subsidiary coinage.[22]

LEGAL TENDER IF STANDARD MONEY CIRCULATES

If the standard money circulates, as it does in a gold coin standard, it should be given the quality of full and unlimited legal tender. This tends to protect both the buyer and the seller in cash transactions, and both debtor and creditor in time transactions. It facilitates settlement of legal disputes and minimizes litigation. In addition, it tends to preserve the standard in fact as well as in law.

Although not absolutely essential, it is generally desirable to have standard money the only full legal tender money, except for small payments. This provision prevents a seller from being pressed to accept any less desirable money—one that is, perhaps, less suitable for storing value until he is ready to utilize it in the purchase of a good or service from someone else. The buyer, too, as long as he offers standard money, is protected against being forced to secure some other money which may be less convenient. In time transactions, the creditor is assured of receiving that money both parties contemplated at the time the contract was made. The debtor knows precisely what money will discharge his debt and terminate litigation. Presumably, justice to both is assured. This assumes, of course, that there is no alteration of the standard during the period of the contract. The standard money is selected as such because, among other reasons, it is a good standard of deferred payments. Varying standards can assure neither justice nor equity to debtor or creditor.

However desirable it may be, it is not absolutely necessary that the standard money be either the actual medium of exchange or the only full legal tender money. But if other forms of money are also full or partial legal tender, safeguards are necessary to prevent the operation of the so-called Gresham's law, and to prevent the development of a dual or multiple monetary standard, in which different prices for the same things are charged depending upon which money, of several, is employed in the payment.[23]

These safeguards include: (1) a limitation on the legal tender quality of money other than the standard (this may include, as will be shown later, use of the legal quality of being receivable for certain specified purposes); (2) limiting the coinage or issuance of money other than the standard; and (3) providing for free, convenient and unlimited conversion and redemption of all moneys into the standard money. Of these, convertibility and redemption are the most effective, but all three may be necessary to insure that the money in actual use adequately represents the standard.

If the convertibility of other forms of money into the standard money is restricted, the effectiveness of the standard unit of measurement of value is greatly reduced. If the conversion is permitted only through a market, with no redemption in the standard money, as for example in the case of United States notes during and after the Civil War to 1879, the irredeemable currency may usurp the functions of the standard money despite its full legal tender quality on the statute books.

When conversion of currencies into the standard money is not limited in any way, it is unwise to designate moneys other than the standard money full legal tender, for no real advantage is obtained. Moneys which are not legal tender, and credit instruments such as checks, have performed and do perform the function of a medium of exchange in an eminently satisfactory manner. A seller or creditor seldom insists on being paid in full legal tender money unless the money offered is inconvenient or its redemption in standard money dubious. Even the infrequent case in which full legal tender money might be demanded involves only a minor inconvenience to the buyer or debtor of converting his money into full legal tender standard money.

The risk and disadvantage of failing to limit the legal tender quality of moneys other than the standard lies in disregarding an important method of control over monetary and fiscal policy by the public. When the legal tender power of these moneys is limited, and doubt arises concerning the worth of a particular kind of money, or concerning the wisdom of government fiscal policies, or banking practices, the limited legal tender money, or non-legal tender money, may be refused. Unusually large returns of such moneys to the banks, or to the government agencies, provide a highly sensitive measure of public confidence.

This highly democratic measure of testing the public approval of fiscal, monetary, and banking policies is an important advantage to be obtained from proper application of the legal tender quality.

LEGAL TENDER IF STANDARD MONEY DOES NOT CIRCULATE

If standard money does not circulate domestically as, for example, under a gold bullion standard, the standard money should not be legal tender because it cannot perform the functions of legal tender. That money which best, and most directly, represents the standard money should be full legal tender under these circumstances. Furthermore, the closest possible relation should be maintained between this representative money and the standard money.

Under a gold bullion standard, for example, if conversion of the representative money into standard money is limited or curtailed, logic requires that the most direct representative of the standard money be protected by the same safeguards as those discussed in the previous section. Moneys other than the direct representative of standard money should have only a limited legal tender quality or none at all. These other moneys should be limited by law as to the amount of their coinage or issue, and they should be freely convertible into the direct representative of standard money. Although these safeguards are more effective when the standard money circulates, applying the same principles to the protection of the representative money as to the standard money maintains a fairly close relationship between the standard money and the media of payment.

If the standard money does not circulate and the direct representative of the standard is also prevented from circulating, the resulting situation is anomalous, illogical, and confusing. If, in addition, both the standard money and the direct representative of standard money are full legal tender, the situation becomes confusion confounded.[24] An analogous situation would arise if a government defined a gallon as 231 cubic inches, provided for the production of gallon containers made of sheet metal, and then passed a law or issued an administrative order forbidding the measurement of liquids in gallons.

LEGAL TENDER AND THE MEANS OF MAKING DEFERRED PAYMENTS

The fundamental reason for the quality of legal tender in money is to designate the means by which deferred payments of all kinds can be measured, and such obligations discharged. To indicate the means or media of discharging such obligations is a necessary legal complement of the recognition and enforcement of contracts between private parties. If, for example, a specific act agreed upon in a contract is not performed, and damages are sustained by one party, the law requires payment of an indemnity. Logically, therefore, there must be some means, sanctioned by law, of satisfying the obligation, or paying the indemnity, or satisfying the judgment, or of preventing further litigation. Designating money legal tender indicates the kind of money legally recognized for such purposes.

One of the fundamental characteristics of a good standard money should be its ability to act as a standard of deferred payments. To do so adequately requires a standard which is as fixed and immutable as is possible.

The question arises: Fixed as to what? Because it cannot be fixed in terms of everything, this must be fixed as to quantities of some things, or some thing, such as weight and fineness of a metal. The same qualities which make a good standard of deferred payments make a good legal tender money. Both justice and logic indicate that the best legal tender money is that thing which would be used to measure deferred payments in the absence of a legal tender law.

There is, of course, a real distinction between selecting a standard of deferred payments and giving the legal tender quality to a particular kind of money. Legal tender is a quality of the means of measurement. If only the standard is legal tender, no change takes place in the legal tender quality without a change in the standard. If money other than the standard is legal tender, a change in the legal tender qualities of such other money does not necessarily mean a change in the standard of deferred payments. Whether or not a change in the standard will occur, depends upon the effectiveness of the safeguards adopted.

Private parties ordinarily rely upon the standard money existing at the time they enter into the contract. They have little choice in the matter, at least in the United States, in view of court interpretations of the effect of legal tender laws. If the obligation is expressed in terms of the monetary unit, such as dollars, without further description, they are relying on the integrity and good faith of the authority which has established a standard of deferred payments and designated the means by which such payments may be made. It follows, therefore, that such authority should change the standard, or alter the relation of the means to the standard, only as a last resort.

PENALTIES AND LEGAL TENDER

The payee is not compelled to accept legal tender when offered, and the law provides no direct penalty for refusing it. As developed in the United States, there exists only an indirect penalty for refusal.

A creditor, for example, may refuse to accept legal tender money for reasons unrelated to the kind of money offered. He may object on grounds that it is insufficient in amount, or that other terms of the contract have not been fulfilled. The law will not support an objection to the kind of money offered, however, if it is made with legal tender money.

In common law there are indirect penalties if legal tender money is offered and refused. The weight of judicial opinion today indicates that, if legal tender is offered *in the proper amount*,[25] and is refused, the interest on the obligation ceases, the burden of the costs is placed upon the one who refuses should he bring suit erroneously. A creditor is compelled to accept legal tender only in the sense that, if he persists in his refusal, the debt eventually will be extinguished through the operation of a statute of limitations.

The effect of a valid tender in law, if rejected, is not to discharge the debt but to enable the debtor to pay the money into court in the event of a legal action on the debt. It allows the debtor to obtain a judgment for the costs of his defense, and the accrual of interest ceases at the time of the tender. A plea of tender, as it is termed in law, is possible in defense of an action of debt, covenant, trespass, trover, slander or libel. On such actions, too, the defendant may bring the legal tender money into court as evidence of his willingness to discharge his obligation or to make amends for his trespass or injury. If the plaintiff refuses to accept the offer thus made, on grounds that the tender is insufficient and proceeds with his suit, and if the damages assessed in the ultimate adjudication are not more than the amount tendered, the plaintiff will not recover his costs and will also pay the defendant's costs.[26]

It is doubtless self-evident that, although only indirect pressure to accept legal tender exists today, there have been other penalties, in the past, upon the seller or creditor who refused to accept legal tender money at its nominal value. Governments have sometimes imposed a long list of various direct and indirect penalties for the failure to accept legal tender. No exhaustive list of penalties is attempted here; they appear to have been limited solely by limitations on human ingenuity.

Roman emperors, for example, are said to have punished the refusal to accept legally coined money by imposing a fine.[27] Fines and imprisonment were inflicted by Henry VIII upon farmers who had the temerity to refuse his coins at the values stated in his proclamations.[28] During the Revolutionary War in America, states assessed various penalties for refusing to accept Continental Currency, some of which strike the student as exceedingly barbaric—ranging from forfeiting the debt, to pillorying, or even the loss of the offender's ears.[29]

LEGAL TENDER AND MEDIA OF EXCHANGE

The importance of legal tender as a quality of the media of

exchange is frequently exaggerated. Some convenience may be added to money used in making payments if it is legal tender, but the quality is by no means essential to the effective performance of that function. In fact, the relative importance of money as a medium of exchange has decreased steadily until today the overwhelming volume of payments in the United States takes place by means of checks which transfer deposit credit.

Ordinarily no question of legal tender is involved when checks are employed. Checks are not legal tender, nor are they money, but written instruments for the transfer of deposit credit. A bank, for example, is not compelled to pay legal tender to the holder of a check. Only the depositor, as a general rule, may compel the bank to pay legal tender, and even this may require a special agreement between the bank and the depositor.[30]

This is clearly illustrated by the case of the *Farmers and Merchants Bank of Monroe, North Carolina, et al. v. Federal Reserve Bank of Richmond, Virginia.* A law passed by the legislature of the State of North Carolina authorized banks operating under its jurisdiction to pay certain specified holders of checks drawn on those banks by means of drafts drawn on their reserve deposits with other banks. The right of the Farmers and Merchants Bank to pay in this manner was upheld despite a contention by the Federal Reserve Bank of Richmond that such a state law violated the Federal Constitution. In rendering its decision the court said:

> "It is contended that in authorizing the payment of checks by a draft drawn on reserve deposits, section 2 violates the provisions of Article I, section 10, clause 1, of the Federal Constitution, which prohibits a State from making anything except gold and silver coin a tender in payment of debts. This claim is clearly unfounded. The debt of the bank is solely to the depositor. The Statute does not authorize the bank to discharge its obligation to its depositor by an exchange draft. It merely provides that, unless the depositor drawing the check specified on its face to the contrary, he shall be deemed to have assented to payment of such a draft."[31]

Prior to 1933, no bank note was legal tender in the United States. Yet these were one of the most important means of payment throughout the nineteenth century and the most important means during the twentieth. It is a long-established rule of law that bank notes, unless they are objected to on grounds of their quality, can perform the function of a medium of exchange without being legal tender. An offer of bank notes, unless specific objection is made, will operate in most respects as if legal tender money had been offered.

This principle is grounded in English common law and in common law in the United States. An early English case, for example, is that of *Wright v. Reed*.[32] The court held that an offer of £100 in Bank of England notes together with notes of various country banks constituted a valid offer to discharge a mortgage although the payee had refused to accept them solely on the grounds that the sum offered was insufficient.

Similarly, in 1796, the plaintiff in an action on a promissory note refused a tender of a £10 note of a country bank on grounds of insufficiency. The court ruled that the objection had been made on quantitative grounds alone and that a failure to object to the kind of money offered constituted a waiver of the plaintiff's right to object on such grounds.[33]

From 1800 to 1863, one finds similar rulings rendered by courts in the United States. During this period notes of banks chartered under the laws of the various states constituted a major part of the currency in circulation. In the case of *Hoyt v. Barnes*,[34] an offer of local bank bills was held to be a valid offer when the payee failed to object to the mode of payment. The bank's notes, which were being redeemed at par at the time the tender was made, and the fact that the plaintiff failed to object to the quality of the money offered at the time, was considered by the court to be a waiver of the right to object to the kind of money offered.[35]

Decisions having the same general effect have been made in federal courts also. In the case of *Griffin et al. v. Thompson,* an offer of bank notes to discharge a promissory note was held to be valid when the payee failed to make specific objection to the kind of money offered. The court said:

"It has been argued that bank notes constitute a good and lawful payment, if received; that, as the law recognizes their circulation, debtors may lawfully tender them in payment, and creditors may lawfully receive them, though not legally bound to do so.

" 'Tis undoubtedly true that the creditor may receive bank notes or blank paper in satisfaction of his debt, for the reason that his power over that debt is supreme, and he may release it without payment of any kind, if he thinks proper."[36]

It appears that bank notes offered and accepted without objection in discharging a debt do not constitute a legal or valid tender unless they are notes of a solvent bank. In 1834, Lightbody offered to pay the Ontario Bank the sum due on his promissory note. The money offered consisted of the notes of an insolvent bank, but was accepted by the Ontario Bank without objection. At the time the tender was made, neither Lightbody nor the Ontario Bank knew of the insolvency. Subsequently the Ontario Bank sued Lightbody for non-payment and the court refused to permit Lightbody's plea that a legal tender had been made.[37]

Similarly in a decision of the United States Supreme Court, in the case of *Ward v. Smith,* Mr. Justice Field stated:

"The doctrine that bank bills are a good tender, unless objected to at the time, only applies to current bills, which are redeemed at the counter of the bank on presentation, and pass at par value in business transactions at the place where offered."[38]

It seems obvious that bank notes should not be made legal tender, for nothing is gained thereby and much is lost. Bank notes are promises to pay legal tender money and, of necessity, involve a debtor-creditor relation. To designate bank notes legal tender confuses the shadow with the substance.

LEGAL TENDER IN CASH TRANSACTIONS

No real difference of kind exists between cash and time

transactions—the difference is solely that of the time interval involved. Nevertheless, it is convenient to divide transactions into those begun and completed at approximately the same time, on the one hand, and those involving a significant time interval between the date of the contract or agreement and the date of the fulfillment or payment, on the other hand. The legal tender quality of money is more significant in time transactions than cash transactions because any change in the legal tender qualities of various moneys may be applicable to debts contracted before the change took place. Sellers, too, may change their prices or alter other conditions of sale to compensate for changes in the legal tender qualities of various moneys—perhaps even setting up differential prices depending on the money involved in payment. If price-fixing enactments have been made, however, the significance of legal tender in cash transactions increases. Under these circumstances, the seller would be deprived of a large part of the protection he enjoys by being able to raise the prices of his goods or services.[39]

This is illustrated by the case of *Atlanta Street Railway Company v. Keeny*. In 1895 Keeny offered a silver half-dollar, dated 1824, in payment of carfare. The coin was genuine although it differed from the half-dollars then in use and was somewhat worn and thin. By the Act of June 9, 1879, Congress had declared such silver coins to be legal tender up to ten dollars in any one payment.[40] After examining the coin, the railway conductor refused to accept it on the grounds that the coin was not good. When the conductor demanded another coin, Keeny refused and was ejected forcibly from the car. In the resulting suit and appeal, Keeny's position was upheld and he was awarded damages. The court held that a genuine silver coin, even if rare and different from most such coins in use, *when legal tender* could be offered in payment of carfare, and a passenger who is ejected for a refusal to make payment otherwise is entitled to damages.[41]

The same principle applies to legal tender coins worn smooth, but still distinguishable,[42] and to a legal tender coin with a hole punched in it but no metal removed.[43]

Withholding the legal tender quality from some of the media

of exchange may serve to protect the seller in cash transactions. The case of *OK Bakery Company v. Morten Milling Company* involved a contract for the delivery of flour by the milling company to the bakery, and required collection on delivery. At the time delivery was made, the bakery offered a check which the agent of the milling company declined to accept. A suit for breach of contract was brought into court by the bakery, but the court sustained the milling company on the grounds that the company had the right to refuse the check because it was not legal tender.[44]

LEGAL TENDER AND SUBSIDIARY COINS

Several principles have been observed in legislative attempts to establish a suitable, convenient, and equitable system of subsidiary coinage. These include: (1) a reduction in the weight of the coin if the same metal as the standard money is used, or the use of a less valuable substance than the standard money, so that the monetary value of the subsidiary coin is sufficiently above its intrinsic value to prevent export or use in industry; (2) a limitation on the amounts coined; (3) a provision for redemption of the coins in standard money on demand; and (4) a limitation on the legal tender quality of the coins.

This study is concerned primarily with the fourth principle. When observed consistently, it provides protection for both payer and payee in both time and cash transactions.[45]

If the legal tender quality of subsidiary coins is not limited, a debt may be paid with large numbers of coins of small denominations. Such a payment may be heavy and cumbersome, and an inconvenience to both the payer and payee. A debtor might legally insist upon making such payments solely for the purpose of annoying his creditor. Merchants might be put to considerable expense and discomfort.

An illustration of the inconvenience which may result if subsidiary coins are unlimited legal tender is provided by the case of *Parrish v. Kohler*.

Kohler was indebted to Parrish for $5,000.00 as evidenced

by a mortgage executed on April 26, 1846. Two years later, at the due date of the mortgage, Kohler offered Parrish 10,000 silver half-dollars. Parrish refused to accept them and demanded that he be paid in coins of a higher denomination or in gold or silver bullion.

The mortgage was executed during a period that silver coins were legal tender for any amount at their nominal value in accordance with an act of Congress in 1837. The act remained in force until February 21, 1853. At that time subsidiary silver coins were made legal tender for sums not exceeding five dollars in one payment.

The court held that Kohler's tender had been a valid one because the coins were full legal tender both at the time the mortgage was executed and at the time the offer was made. Interest ceased at the date of the tender and Parrish paid the defendant's costs as well as his own.[46]

Limiting the legal tender quality of subsidiary coins may be accomplished, as Neil Carothers has carefully pointed out,[47] either by limiting the number of coins which may be used in one payment or by limiting the value of the coins in one payment. Of the two methods, the former is much the better because it is more precise. Coinage laws of the United States, however, have used the latter method exclusively.

Even if the legal tender quality of subsidiary coins is limited by either of the two methods, a debtor bent on wilfully causing annoyance could probably do so. This is illustrated by the case of *Boatman's Savings Institution v. Bank of the State of Missouri.*[48] The Bank of the State of Missouri was anxious to maintain its notes in circulation and to avoid depleting its cash reserves by redeeming its notes in legal tender gold or silver coin. To discourage redemption, the Bank contended that each of its circulating notes (ranging in denomination from five to fifty dollars) was a separate and distinct demand. It proceeded to tender, on each bill presented, five dollars in subsidiary silver coin, which were legal tender up to five dollars in any one payment, and the balance in gold coins or full legal tender silver dollars. When brought into court, the court sustained the plea that a tender had been made and that each bank note presented for payment was a separate and distinct demand.

The remedy for this lies outside questions of the legal qualities of money and in the realm of general banking legislation to prevent such practices.

LEGAL TENDER AND REVENUES OF THE STATE

One of the most frequently observed purposes in making certain moneys legal tender has been to secure additional revenues for the state or the ruler. Legal tender, because of its importance to both debtor and creditor, is a quality eminently suited to modify the debt burden of absolute authority although its economic effects are quite a different matter. From earliest times, rulers appear to have seized avidly upon the device of devaluing coins, enforcing their acceptance at the former rates and thus increasing their revenues, or reducing their outstanding debts, or both. The coinage operations of Henry VIII and Edward VI, together with their proclamations, undoubtedly had this purpose.[49]

To secure revenues or reduce debt was doubtless a major reason for making Continental Currency a legal tender. The same observation applies to the paper money of the American colonies and individual states, and to the United States notes of the Civil War period. One is tempted to raise the further question of what fundamental difference, if any, exists between these earlier devaluations and the present monetization of the federal debt.

Certainly it is difficult, if not impossible, to defend the use of the legal tender quality for such ulterior purposes on moral grounds. Logically, expediency would seem the only valid defense. It can easily be observed that the practice has been condemned by our most outstanding monetary economists for more than a century—with something less than brilliant success.

John Stuart Mill described such actions in these words:

" . . . Profligate governments . . . until a very modern period, seldom scrupled, for the sake of robbing their creditors, to confer on all debtors a license to rob theirs, by the shallow and impudent device of lowering the standard; that least covert of all modes of knavery, which consists in calling a shilling a pound, that a debt of one hundred pounds may be cancelled by the payment of a hundred shillings. It would have been as simple a plan, and would have answered the purpose as well, to have enacted that 'a hundred' should always be interpreted to mean five, which would have effected the same reduction of all pecuniary contracts, and would not have been at all more shameless. Such strokes of policy have not wholly ceased to be recommended, but they have ceased to be practiced; except occasionally through the medium of paper money, in which case the character of the transaction, from the greater obscurity of the subject, is a little less barefaced."[50]

LEGAL TENDER TO FAVOR DEBTORS OR CREDITORS

The legal tender quality has been given to money from time to time in order to favor either debtors or creditors as a class. In 1786 the Rhode Island legislature came to be controlled by a farmer-debtor party favoring the issuance of large sums in legal tender paper money. Almost immediately after taking office, its members passed a law requiring the issuance of $100,000 in paper bills of credit. The act made the bills legal tender for all debts except those owed to charitable institutions. One historian describes the operation of the law as follows:

"The law acted as a general liquidation law. If a creditor refused to receive the bills in payment of his claim, the debtor made immediate application to a justice . . . who issued a citation to the creditor to appear at his dwelling house in ten days and receive the money as prescribed by law. The judge . . . , in case the creditor failed or refused to call for the money within the specified time, advertised the facts in the newspaper three weeks and the debtor was discharged of his debt."[51]

Apparently the worthy Yankees of Rhode Island could not bring themselves to subject charitable institutions to the same treatment as that given to other creditors.

Similarly, although more subtly written, the Thomas Amendment to the Agricultural Adjustment Act of May 12, 1933, which had as one of its purposes making all money of the United States full legal tender, seems to have had as an additional purpose the favoring of debtors as a class.[52] The amendment's author, Senator Thomas, addressed his colleagues on April 24, 1933, as follows:

> "Mr. President, it will be my task to show that, if the Amendment shall prevail, it has potentialities as follows:
>
> "It may transfer from one class to another class in these United States value to the extent of almost $200,000,000,000. This value will be transferred first from those who own the bank deposits; secondly, this value will be transferred from those who own bonds and fixed investments. If the Amendment carries and the powers are exercised in reasonable degree, it must transfer that $200,000,000,000 in the hands of persons who now have it, who did not buy it, who did not earn it, who do not deserve it, who must not retain it, back to the other side, the debtor class of the Republic, the people who owe the mass of debts of the nation. . . ."[53]

Examples of the use of the legal tender quality to favor creditors as a class are observed less frequently. Apparently the image of the creditor as a grasping, conniving holder of the mortgage on the old homestead, plus the fact that the government is normally a debtor, prevents much of the special purpose legislation on the creditor's behalf. Changes in the weight or fineness of the standard money normally have been accompanied by changes in the legal tender quality of money. Most frequently, however, the changes have been reductions in either weight or fineness, or both, which tend to favor debtors rather than creditors. Whatever legislation might be said to be generally favorable to the creditor has been that aimed at restricting the legal tender quality of money and the maintenance of the monetary standard over a period of time against efforts at devaluation.

A British law of 1774 may have favored creditors whether purposely or incident to its other purposes. From 1717 to 1774 English silver coins were legal tender at their nominal value without limit.[54] After 1764, however, the importation of underweight silver coins which had worn thin from use in foreign trade seems to have increased in a modified application of Gresham's principle. Full weight coins tended to find their way into foreign trade while the poorer coins returned to domestic payments where no discrimination against them was legally possible. On May 10, 1774, the House of Commons passed a resolution which read:

" . . . No tender in the payment of money made in the silver coin of the realm, of any sum exceeding the sum of £25 at any one time, shall be reputed in law or allowed to be a legal tender within Great Britain or Ireland for more than according to its weight, after the rate of 5s. 2d. per oz. of silver. . . . "[55]

Thus, before 1774, a debtor was permitted to pay his debt in silver coin, irrespective of the amount of the debt or the weight of the coin. After that date, however, although the debt could still be paid in silver the portion of the debt in excess of £25 could only be paid in silver valued by weight instead of the face or nominal value of the coins. Although the purposes of the legislation were to protect the standard of value and to prevent clipping of coin, it was also favorable to creditors whose claims were in large amounts. Apparently, too, the mint price of silver prior to this act had been higher, thus benefiting the creditor in another way.[56]

There seems to be no moral justification for employing a legal tender law to favor any particular class or group in a society —whether the group is composed of debtors or creditors is somewhat beside the point. In addition to the fact that individuals are usually both debtors and creditors at the same time, to compel a man to accept less than that to which he is entitled, or to pay more than he would be compelled to pay in the absence of a legal tender law, are both inequitable and unjust acts. In the event that class legislation be undertaken under politically expedient circumstances, it should be effected directly rather than by the subterfuge of altering the legal tender quality of money.

LEGAL TENDER AND THE VALUE OF MONEY

Money has sometimes been designated legal tender in the belief, whether expressed explicitly or not, that this increases or maintains the "value" of money. Although there are many assertions in the literature to the effect that this is so, this author has found no objective evidence to support the statement.

Part of the difficulty may be found in the very obscurity of the phrase "value of money," which has several possible meanings and is often employed somewhat carelessly. As the phrase is used in the Constitution of the United States,[57] it means the weight and fineness of the monetary unit in terms of some thing or things, such as the number of grains of gold of a particular fineness. This is essentially a weight concept.[58]

The phrase has also been employed to mean the value of a given money in terms of other money, domestic or foreign, such as a foreign exchange rate, or a gold dollar in terms of United States notes during the greenback money period of 1862 to 1879.

"Value" of money may also mean the "purchasing power" of money, which itself is a vague term. This may mean its value, or purchasing power, in terms of one or more goods which a unit of money can buy, or even a statistical estimate of the amounts of *all* goods and services which a unit of money can buy. In this latter sense the value of money becomes the reciprocal of a price index number—itself a more or less imperfect measure of the general purchasing power of a unit of money.

Legal tender can have no relation to the value of money in the first meaning. "Value" in this sense of the word is solely a question of legal definition. If the value of a dollar is 15 and 5/21 grains of gold, this value cannot be changed by addition or omission of the legal tender quality.

In the second meaning it is possible that the legal tender quality may exert an indirect influence upon the value of money.

If a money is made legal tender, a demand for that money to be used where legal tender is required *may* be created. This does not mean that such a demand *must* be created. Even if the demand were to increase significantly solely because of the addition of the legal tender quality to a particular money, if the supply of that money were increased at the same time, the influence of the increased demand for the money may be offset or exceeded.

When the value of money refers to purchasing power in terms of some goods or all goods, the quality of being legal tender is of negligible importance compared to other factors, such as costs, tastes, incomes, habits, etc., which influence the demand for and supply of goods. This is illustrated clearly by the experience with Continental Currency, state paper money, and United States notes.

Despite the fact that the legal tender quality of a money can have only an insignificant influence on the value of money, the belief that legal tender gives value to money has persisted for hundreds of years. From time to time in legislative debates one finds various versions of the argument presented by John Law in 1720[59]—logic and experience to the contrary notwithstanding. In a more obscure form, the same unfounded belief may be observed in various forms of fiat money theories and in the equally unwarranted belief in the efficacy of direct price control.

There is not space, in this study, to catalogue the monotonous arguments relative to purchasing power and the legal qualities of money. The belief, however erroneous it may be, has remained an important factor in laws concerning legal tender.[60]

C
LAWFUL MONEY

TWO MEANINGS OF LAWFUL MONEY

Two distinct legal qualities of money in American practice

are described by the same words: lawful money. One is a broad and general quality describing all money properly issued by appropriate legal authority, such as government coin, paper money, and bank notes legally issued. The second quality is more technical and narrower than the first, describing the *kind* of money which may properly be used in reserves against notes or deposits of banking institutions, or in redeeming other kinds of money. This technical meaning of the words appears to have evolved from the use of the term in state and federal legislation regulating the monetary and banking system. The history of the phrase, lawful money, is described on pages 67-71; 87-93.

Money is lawful in the broad sense because it has a legal sanction or recognition of some kind. Lawful money in this broad sense means all money which is not *unlawful*. Unlawful money may be divided into: (1) counterfeit money; (2) money which has been issued by an illegal government such as the paper money of the Confederate States during the American Civil War;[61] (3) money illegally issued by a legal government; (4) bank notes illegally issued; and (5) privately issued coins, tokens, scrip, trade certificates, etc.

With a few minor exceptions, this study is concerned primarily with lawful money in the technical sense. In this sense the words are usually used without other description and refer to money which has been declared lawful by appropriate authorities for certain specific uses. Lawful money is a legal quality of money designating money which may be used in one or more of the following ways: (1) as a reserve against bank deposits; (2) as a reserve against bank notes outstanding; (3) as a reserve against government paper money; and (4) as a means of redeeming government paper money or bank notes.

ORIGIN AND EVOLUTION OF LAWFUL MONEY

The technical concept of lawful money developed concomitantly with the increase in the complexity of the monetary and banking structure during the nineteenth century. Two factors appear to have induced the use of the term: first, an increase in the number and kinds of money; and second, an increased use of deposit banking with transfers of deposits, represented by checks and drafts, performing most of the functions of a medium of exchange.

During the American colonial period, the term lawful money appears to have been popularly employed to describe the kind of money in which certain other moneys, or bills of credit, would be redeemed. In the first half of the nineteenth century, state laws used the term to designate the kind of money to be used by banks chartered under state authority as reserves against their circulating notes or deposit liabilities. After 1862, a similar use of the term is found in federal legislation. The words appear in legislation governing the national bank system, the Federal Reserve System, and the Postal Savings System.

LAWFUL MONEY IN RESERVES AND REDEMPTION FUNDS

Lawful money is most closely related to the function of money as a reserve against notes and deposits. In this function, four purposes of reserves are distinguishable: (1) to limit the amount, by value, of notes issuable; (2) to limit the amount of bank credit extension; (3) to provide the means of discharging liability for notes and deposits; and (4) to facilitate the clearing of credit balances. Redemption funds are reserves against paper money notes, the principal purpose of which is to provide the means of discharging liability for such notes.

The control of bank credit, bank note issue, and government paper money issue has both qualitative and quantitative aspects. The first two purposes of reserves mentioned above are essentially quantitative; the third and fourth purposes are qualitative. To designate certain money as "lawful money" for reserve purposes is one method of controlling the quality of reserves; lawful money thus concerns the proper kinds of money to comprise assets or reserves against certain liabilities. It is a question of proper accounting procedure, and of proper and logical control of banking operations and the nation's monetary structure.

CHARACTERISTICS OF LAWFUL MONEY

Money designated "lawful money" by statute or administrative authority, for use in reserves and redemption funds, should have characteristics suited to the purposes of reserves. Uncertainty as to the future induces men to create reserves as insurance against unforeseen, or inaccurately foreseeable, contingencies. Lawful money, therefore, should consist of money capable of storing value over time.

To function as a limit upon the amount of notes issued, or the amount of credit extended, requires that lawful money be relatively scarce. If it is available in unlimited quantities, or even relatively large quantities, it cannot successfully fulfill this purpose.

To fulfill the third and fourth purposes of reserves, lawful money should be capable of discharging the liability against which it is held. Preferably, therefore, it should be convenient and easily transferable.

All standard money should be lawful money, but it is not necessary that the standard money be the only lawful money. Logically, the standard money is selected because it can discharge obligations, both domestically and in foreign trade; because it is a good storehouse of value; because it is relatively scarce; and other reasons. These characteristics of standard money usually coincide with the desirable characteristics of lawful money and, for this reason, all standard money should be lawful money. Money other than the standard money may possess some of the desired characteristics of lawful money also, and there is no reason to exclude such money from use as reserves or in the redemption of paper currency.

LAWFUL MONEY AND LEGAL TENDER

Certain opinions to the contrary, legal tender and lawful money are not identical qualities. Legal tender money is not necessarily lawful money, nor is lawful money necessarily legal tender.[62] Full legal tender money may be used in any payment within the jurisdiction of the authority capable of so designating money, provided always that the laws are consistent. As a general rule, legal tender money should also be lawful money. But relative scarcity, or ability to store value, or even logical consistency or accounting principles, may be the governing characteristics. Gold may be a more appropriate money than legal tender paper money for some reserve purposes, for example, if a country adopts a gold bullion standard. In the United States, money has been lawful money without being legal tender and, less frequently, legal tender without being lawful money.

LAWFUL MONEY AT THE PRESENT TIME

Today questions involving the nature and significance of lawful money arise in connection with determining the kinds of money which may be used for the following purposes: (1) by the Federal Reserve banks as reserves against deposit liabilities; (2) by banks which are not members of the Federal Reserve System against deposit liabilities; (3) by the Treasury of the United States as reserves against deposits in the Postal Savings Banks; (4) by the Treasury and the Federal Reserve banks to redeem Federal Reserve notes; (5) by a Federal Reserve bank for deposit with its Federal Reserve agent to reduce its liability for Federal Reserve notes outstanding; (6) by a Federal Reserve bank to reimburse the five percent redemption fund held by the Treasury to redeem Federal Reserve notes; (7) as money to retire national bank notes; and (8) as money to retire Federal Reserve bank notes.

D

MONEY RECEIVABLE FOR SPECIFIED PURPOSES

MEANING OF MONEY RECEIVABLE

By state or federal law money may be designated "receivable" for specified purposes. These purposes have included: (1) payments of all kinds by private persons to a government; (2) payments of all kinds by a government to private persons; (3) payments by private persons to corporations or associations existing by the authority of government.

For example, Treasury notes authorized by the Act of Congress February 25, 1813,[63] were declared to be "receivable in payments of all duties and taxes laid by authority of the United States and of all public lands sold by the said authority." This is the most common type of clause used in federal statutes to designate certain money receivable in payments of private persons to governments.[64]

A more inclusive type of receivability clause appeared in the Act of June 3, 1864, which amended the National Bank Act.[65] Section 23 of the amended act states that national bank notes ". . . shall be received *at par* in all parts of the United States in payment of taxes, excises, public lands and all other dues to the United States, except for duties on imports, and also for all salaries and other debts and demands owing by the United States to individuals, corporations, and associations within the United States, except interest on the public debt and in redemption of the national currency." This act also provided, in Section 32, that: "Every association formed or existing under the provisions of this act shall take and receive at par for any liability to the said association any and all notes or bills issued by any association existing under and by virtue of this act." Thus the acceptance of national bank notes at par by any national bank was made a specific condition for the formation of such an association.

LEGAL EFFECT OF RECEIVABILITY

When money is designated receivable for specified purposes, no other money may be preferred legally for such purposes. It is not compulsory to use such money alone for the purposes specified, but no other money may be recognized by law as superior. Other kinds of money may be offered and accepted for the purposes specified, provided the use of such money is not prohibited by law.

A refusal to accept money receivable for specified purposes, provided the law has not been repealed or amended, has the same legal effect as a refusal to accept legal tender money. A plea of tender may be entered in defense of a legal action for non-payment. Money receivable for specified purposes is thus similar to limited legal tender money, with limitations upon the kind of payment rather than its amount.

In two kinds of payments, however, legal tender money may be preferred and legally demanded: (1) those involving a debtor-creditor relation between private persons; and (2) those involving a buyer-seller relation between private persons.[66] Money made receivable in other kinds of payments *may* be used in the two payments above also, but the payee may refuse to accept it and can insist on payment in legal tender money without penalty of any kind. For these two kinds of payments, money receivable for other purposes has no greater recognition than money which is neither receivable for any purpose nor legal tender.

The legal effect of paying money which has been designated receivable for specified purposes is clearly established. In *Thorndike v. United States,* the Supreme Court decided that Treasury notes which had been designated receivable by the Treasury in payments to the United States could be legally used in such payments, and that an offer of the notes could be pleaded as a valid tender on such debts.[67] Similarly, notes of a state chartered bank which, according to state law, were to be "received in payment of all debts due to the State of Arkansas," were given the same effect as legal tender when offered in payment of such debts.[68]

That money made receivable for specified payments *may* be used in any payment has also been clearly decided. In *Veazie Bank v. Fenno* the Supreme Court decided that national bank notes, which were receivable for certain purposes and not legal tender, were made "fit for use by those who see fit to use them in all the transactions of commerce."[69] In *MacLeod v. Hoover,*[70] the court decided that Federal Reserve notes and Federal Reserve bank notes, receivable for purposes specified in the Federal Reserve Act, could be refused on grounds that they were not legal tender. If they are refused on grounds other than that of quality, however, the right to insist upon payment in legal tender is deemed to have been waived. This is not different from the long-standing rule of law concerning bank notes in general, irrespective of whether or not such notes are receivable for any purpose whatsoever.

RECEIVABILITY AND LAWFUL MONEY

All money which has been designated receivable for some purpose is lawful money in the broad sense. However, in the technical sense of money lawful for reserve purposes, there is no necessary relation between money receivable for specified purposes and lawful money.

FOOTNOTES

[1] See, for example, the excellent treatment in W. W. Carlile, *The Evolution of Modern Money* (The Macmillan Company, London, 1901); also William Ridgeway, *The Origin of Metallic Currency and Weight Standards* (Cambridge University Press, Cambridge, England, 1892) and A. R. Burns, *Money and Monetary Policy in Early Times* (Alfred A. Knopf, New York, 1927).

[2] Terminology differs but the following are representative: Walter E. Spahr and others, *Economic Principles and Problems* (Farrar and Rinehart, Inc., New York, 1940), 4th ed., Vol. I, pp. 438-441; J. Marvin Peterson and Delmas R. Cawthorne, *Money and Banking* (The Macmillan Company, New York, 1949), pp. 10-14; Charles R. Whittlesey, *Principles and Practices of Money and Banking* (The Macmillan Company, New York, 1954), pp. 10-12; Charles L. Prather, *Money and Banking* (Richard D. Irwin, Inc., Homewood, Illinois, 1953), pp. 14-20.

[3] A particularly thoughtful, and therefore unusual, discussion of monetary functions may be found in H. L. Reed, *Money, Currency, and Banking* (McGraw-Hill Book Company, Inc., New York, 1942), Chapter I. It is earnestly recommended to the serious student.

⁴ *The World Almanac and Book of Facts for 1948* (New York World-Telegram, New York, 1948), p. 637.

⁵ Professors Graham and Whittlesey in their *Golden Avalanche* (Princeton University Press, Princeton, New Jersey, 1939, p. 215) have asserted that money has become less concrete and more representative and abstract over time. The student should be wary because of the wide definition of money employed. While this is true of the medium of exchange, it does not appear to be true of standard money. Views such as those of Graham, Whittlesey, and others should be compared with those of Kemmerer, Ridgeway, Rist, Reed, Spahr, Conant, Laughlin, and many others.

⁶ Those particularly interested in expanding the history of tender in this sense should examine Alva R. Hunt, *A Treatise on the Law of Tender and Bringing Money into Court* (Frank P. Dufresne, St. Paul, Minnesota, 1903), *passim*. Hunt, unfortunately, was not trained in monetary economics. The student must supplement Hunt, therefore, with Henry Dunning MacLeod, *The History of Economics* (Bliss, Sands and Co., London, 1896).

⁷ Little is to be gained by extensive citation on this point. The reader should examine textbooks of the 1890-1930 period particularly for examples of this assertion. Current practice is to assert that it is not necessarily a property of the standard money.

⁸ For two authorities who saw this clearly but who state it somewhat differently, see Reed, *op. cit.*, Appendix I, and Ludwig von Mises, *The Theory of Money and Credit* (Harcourt, Brace and Co., Inc., New York, 1935), pp. 68ff. One must always remember, when reading Mises, that he uses the term "money" somewhat differently than most writers, then substitutes the rather awkward, but very descriptive, phrase "money-substitutes."

⁹ W. A. Bewes, *The Romance of the Law Merchant* (Sweet and Maxwell, Ltd., London, 1923), pp. 50-52.

¹⁰ The evolution of monetary standards is described in some detail in MacLeod, *op. cit.*, pp. 360-369.

¹¹ *Articles of Confederation*, Article IX.

¹² In 1830, Chief Justice Marshall observed that the Continental Congress "did not, and perhaps could not, make bills of credit legal tender." (*Craig v. Missouri*, 4 Peters 110.) The authority of the Continental Congress relative to the legal qualities of money is discussed on pages 22-23.

¹³ 15 & 16 Geo. V, c. 29 (1925).

¹⁴ American legislation is illogical and misleading on this point. Current laws, inconsistencies, and confusion are discussed on pages 109-126.

¹⁵ Theodor Mommsen, *Histoire de la Monnaie Romaine* (Rollin and Feuardent, Paris, 1865), Vol. I, p. 173.

¹⁶ Sophonisba P. Breckinridge, *Legal Tender: A Study in British and American Monetary History* (University of Chicago Press, Chicago,

1903), pp. 18-22.

[17] Charles Jenkinson, 1st Earl of Liverpool, *A Treatise on the Coins of the Realm* (E. Wilson, London, 1880), p. 21. It should be noted that the commonly accepted conditions of a bimetallic standard were present: (1) unlimited coinage of both metals; (2) a fixed ratio between the metals; and (3) both metals "legal tender" (that is to say, that both had equal recognition in the royal proclamations). Logically, it is unnecessary to have the third.

[18] It seems probable, in view of our subsequent experience with monetary standards, that a silver standard could have been restored by limiting gold coinage and providing for redemption of the gold coins in silver—even if equal recognition (both coins legal tender) had been maintained. There can be no doubt, for example, that the United States maintained a gold coin standard under the Act of March 14, 1900, although silver dollars as well as gold coins were full legal tender.

[19] The statistics, as might be expected, are meager. But the general results are indicated in W. A. Shaw, *The History of Currency 1252-1894* (G. P. Putnam's Sons, New York, 1896), 2nd ed., p. 11; Liverpool, *op. cit.,* p. 46.

[20] England was on a paper standard, in fact if not in law, from 1797 to 1821. Although this legislation was passed in 1816, redemption of paper notes in gold did not begin until 1821. The period is described in greater detail in Edwin W. Kemmerer, *Gold and the Gold Standard* (McGraw-Hill Book Company, Inc., New York, 1944), p. 41.

[21] 56 Geo. III, c. 68 (1816).

[22] William Graham, *The One Pound Note in the History of Banking in Great Britain* (J. Thin, Edinburgh, 1911), pp. 87-88.

[23] There are many historical examples of systems having more than one currency, some or all of which were legal tender, in which the cheaper or cheapest tended to supplant the dearer or dearest. When the cheaper is government paper money, it has often become the standard money in fact, if not in law. In this case, gold and silver tend to become commodities, the prices of which fluctuate in terms of the paper money in the same manner as the prices of other commodities. With only minor modifications, this applies to the United States during the period of the Greenbacks. Many other such systems are described in detail by Edwin Walter Kemmerer in *Modern Currency Reforms* (The Macmillan Company, New York, 1916), pp. 245-292.

[24] This circumstance, which exists under the present monetary laws of the United States, is discussed on pp. 112-113.

[25] This indicates why a refusal to accept a bill larger than two dollars at a subway change booth, for example, does not involve a question of legal tender. The objection is to the quantity and not the quality of the money.

[26] Hunt, *op. cit., passim;* Sidney Webster, *The Misuse of Legal Tender* (D. Appleton and Company, New York, 1893), pp. 14-16.

27 Charles A. Pellat, *Textes Choisis des Pandectes* (E. Giard, Paris, 1859), p. 75. The student will find many other examples in Pellat's work.

28 Henry Dunning McLeod, *The Theory and Practice of Banking* (Bliss, Sands and Co., London, 1855), Vol. I, p. 103.

29 A. Barton Hepburn, *A History of Coinage in the United States* (The Macmillan Company, New York, 1924), pp. 17-19.

30 A short list of cases concerning the development of this general rule before 1903 is given in Hunt, *op. cit.*, pp. 81-84.

31 262 U.S. 649 (1923).

32 3 T.R. 554 (1790).

33 *Lockyer v. Jones,* Peak 180 (1796). Similar rulings may be found by other English courts in *Tiley v. Courtier,* 2 C. & J. 16 (1817); *Grigby v. Oakes et al.,* 2 B. & P. 526 (1801); *Polglass v. Olivier,* 2 C. & J. 15 (1831).

34 11 Me. 475 (1834).

35 Similar decisions may be found in the courts of other states; for example, *M'Eowen v. Rose,* 5 N.J.L. 582 (1819) and *MacLeod v. Hoover,* 159 La. 244, 105 So. 305 (1925).

36 2 How. 249 (1844).

37 *Ontario Bank v. Lightbody,* 13 Wend. (N.Y.) 101 (1834).

38 7 Wall. 447 (1868).

39 If I understand Mises correctly, I would disagree with his observations on this point [Ludwig von Mises, *The Theory of Money and Credit* (Harcourt, Brace and Co., Inc., New York, 1935), pp. 69-71]. His position seems to be that legal tender laws affect only obligations which have already been contracted. This in turn seems to stem from the idea that the law regards money "only as a means of cancelling outstanding obligations" (p. 69). The fact is, at least in American monetary history, that legal tender laws *do* affect cash transactions and the law *does* regard money having the legal tender quality as money of importance for other purposes than cancelling outstanding obligations.

40 21 *Statutes at Large* 7.

41 99 Ga. 266; 25 S.E. 629; 33 L.R.A. 824 (1896).

42 *Jersey City and Bergen Railroad v. Morgan,* 160 U.S. 288 (1895).

43 *United States v. Lissner,* 12 Fed. Rep. 840 (1882).

44 141 S.W. (Tex.) 436 (1940).

45 The reasons for the first three principles, and their significance, are discussed in detail in the *Report of the Monetary Commission of the Indianapolis Convention of Boards of Trade, Chambers of Commerce, Commercial Clubs and other similar bodies of the United States* (The Hallenbeck Press, Indianapolis, Indiana, 1898), pp. 113-123.

46 11 Phila. (Pa.) 346 (1856).

47 *Fractional Money* (John Wiley and Sons, Inc., New York, 1930).

48 33 Mo. 497 (1863).

49 Rogers Ruding, *Annals of the Coinage of Britain and Its Dependencies*

from the Earliest Period to the Reign of Queen Victoria (John Hearne, London, 1840), Vol. II, p. 74; Liverpool, *op. cit.*, p. 41. To extend the list of citations would serve no useful purpose, for it is quite generally recognized as an unfortunate practice which, despite our knowledge and presumed superior morality, persists in one form or another to the present.

[50] *Principles of Political Economy*, Sir W. J. Ashley, ed. (Longmans, Green and Co., New York, 1909), pp. 486-487. The paragraph was written a century ago. Mill can be criticized perhaps, for his over-optimism concerning the moral rejuvenation of governments.

[51] Charles J. Bullock, *Essays on the Monetary History of the United States* (The Macmillan Company, New York, 1900), pp. 193-194.

[52] The legal tender provisions of this Act are discussed on page 109.

[53] *Congressional Record,* Vol. 77, p. 2217.

[54] Liverpool, *op. cit.,* p. 94; Carlile, *op. cit.,* p. 72.

[55] Ruding, *op. cit.,* Vol. IV, p. 33.

[56] Liverpool, *op. cit.,* p. 94.

[57] Section 8. "The Congress shall have Power . . . to coin Money, regulate the Value thereof, and of foreign Coin, and fix the Standard of Weights and Measures. . . ."

[58] The legal value of the dollar today, for example, is 15 and 5/21 grains of gold, 9/10 fine.

[59] "The majority of men will surely say that the credit of a particular note is based on and maintained by the freedom to accept or reject it; on the contrary, I am of the opinion that the credit of this note is in doubt and its circulation limited, precisely because its acceptance is left free. . . . If everybody were compelled to accept the note, it might never be returned at all, and the issuer might never be compelled to redeem it." From John Law's *Troisième Lettre sur le Nouveau Système des Finances* (1720), quoted in Charles Rist, *History of Monetary and Credit Theory from John Law to the Present Day* (The Macmillan Company, London, 1940), p. 64.

[60] American experience demonstrated, incontrovertibly, that the legal tender quality of money does not, in itself, maintain or increase the value of money in any accepted meaning of the phrase. A few examples are given in the historical section of this study; other examples of the lack of relationship of legal tender and the value of money are given by Wesley C. Mitchell in *A History of Greenbacks* (University of Chicago Press, Chicago, 1903).

[61] This is often determinable only *after* the fact, for certainly the Confederate notes were lawful when issued. Furthermore, unlawful money of this kind may be given a limited legal status even after it has been determined to be unlawful. Two cases in which the courts gave some legal standing in private contracts to Confederate notes are *Thorington v. Smith,* 75 U.S. 1 (1869); and *Hanover v. Woodruff,* 82 U.S. 439 (1872).

[62] The statement refers to American law only. It is this misunderstanding that put Miss Breckinridge, and apparently Professor Laughlin also, on the wrong track. Had the study undertaken in 1903 waited another ten years or so, this might have been avoided. Courts, too, have contributed to the error.

[63] 2 *Statutes at Large* 801.

[64] The wording of the statutes varies considerably. A history of the concept is given on pages 63-67; 82-87.

[65] 13 *Statutes at Large* 99.

[66] The fact that national bank notes, for example, were designated receivable at par for all debts to national banking associations is not a true exception to this rule. These associations were chartered by the federal government; the requirement that the banks receive these notes was a specific condition of the statute by virtue of which the associations existed. There is a similar clause in the Federal Reserve Act relative to Federal Reserve notes.

[67] 2 Mason 1 (1819).

[68] *Woodruff v. Trapnall,* 51 U.S. 190 (1850).

[69] 75 U.S. 533 (1869).

[70] 159 La. 244 (1925).

chapter

8

RECOMMENDATIONS

It is incumbent upon those who criticize particular legislation, or who imply that a given situation is inconsistent and illogical, not only to state the principles governing the proper remedy but also to present a specific plan of action. But it is exactly at this point that most disagreement will be found—regardless of general agreement on principle.

In attempting to present recommendations which, if adopted, would provide a just and proper utilization of the legal qualities of money, the serious investigator departs from an explanation of that which is and enters upon a discussion of that which should be. Proper utilization of the qualities of legal tender, lawful money, and money receivable for specified purposes presupposes a decision as to the nature of the basic monetary system. But the nature of the monetary system is dependent, at least in part, upon the nature of the entire politico-economic structure. What recommendations are made by the author in this chapter, therefore, will be criticized severely by others or perhaps disregarded not so much because of the monetary principles but because of the political convictions involved. These political convictions, moreover, are usually beyond logical argument. There are economists who believe in the desirability of a planned or directed economy. These should favor, if they are logical, utilizing planned money for social ends. Their use of the legal qualities of money ought to be quite different from that of economists who believe in an economically free economy, with an autonomous price mechanism, and limited government.

Three broad plans are conceivable, any one of which would remove the logical inconsistencies which are to be noted in our present use of these legal qualities. They lead, however, in different political directions. One such plan involves the formalization of that monetary system which we appear to have adopted in fact while denying it in words; namely, an inconvertible paper money standard. This would have the advantage, at least, of drawing attention to the issues involved and place the ultimate responsibility for the results. It would remove the government from the requirement of paying for its borrowings a rate of interest equal to that which other borrowers must pay. Draw aside the curtains which hide these monetary maneuverings and it will become plain to all that this has, in fact, been happening for quite a period of time.

Except for certain uses of the lawful money quality in reserves and redemption funds, an inconvertible paper money standard would make few changes in the legal qualities of money. All money, being paper and without intrinsic value, should be full legal tender except for small coins. In considering these, even an inconvertible paper money system ought to set some standards for limitation of the legal tender quality. No money needs to be lawful money, nor receivable for particular purposes. Since there would be no redemption of money, use of the lawful money concept would be quite redundant. All money would be equally good—and equally bad—and other forms of government debt would be eliminated save that of money. The annoying and painful necessity of finding the means of paying for worth-while government expenditures would be eliminated. Expensive subterfuges, or vestigial remains of the superstition of government solvency, would be eliminated. Any stocks of gold or silver could be sold to the highest bidder and, as long as they were kept within the country, could be repurchased at any time with newly printed money by the government. Paper money issued by Federal Reserve banks, in the form of Federal Reserve notes, would be unnecessary. Paper money would be put into circulation as the government needed spending money, or merely deposited in the Federal Reserve banks, and transferred from person to person by means of deposit credit. In fact, as long as such credit continued to be accepted, there would be no need for paper money at all—except for properly engraved certificates to the effect that "This Is One Dollar." With no limitation on issue of these bills, the government could buy any business it desired by paying the owners their price. The lack of limitation would also make possible an indefinite amount of capital supplied to producers of anything which the government considered desirable. The Secretary of the Treasury could avoid the annoying restrictions imposed by the necessity of refunding operations by paying off the government debt in paper money, although Congress might prefer to retain the fiction that such debts might be paid at some other future time.

There are those who think this illustration is overexaggerated. The author does not believe it to be so. Basically, the issue is one of morals and, if the question is faced squarely, few can demonstrate any restraint upon government under a monetary standard composed of inconvertible paper money. That this is so, and that the issue is a moral one, is demonstrated by the fact that we retain the fictions concerning the relationship of our money to gold. Federal Reserve notes promise to pay, to redeem; United States notes promise to pay, to redeem. We are unwilling to say, "This Is One Dollar," because we fear such a statement might give rise to repudiation, refusal to accept the money, doubt of its future worth, and all kinds of other disturbances. One piece of paper becomes the security for another. Several months ago the crowning faith in the efficacy of paper occurred when it was revealed that the federal government had stockpiled, over a period of time, some billions of dollars worth of paper money as a hedge against the possibility that enemy bombers might destroy the means of producing it. Instead of dispersing the substance, the gold reserves, these are centralized while the shadow is carefully preserved, protected, and dispersed.

If, then, we disregard the adoption of an inconvertible paper money standard as a remedy for the existing inconsistencies, there appear to be two other possible solutions: either the restoration of a gold coin standard; or the adoption of a gold bullion standard. This author believes the adoption of a gold coin standard, including consistent application of the legal qualities of money to preserve it, constitutes the best method of restoring logic to our present monetary and banking structure. Such action would require the following:

1. The laws making all coins and currencies of the United States legal tender should be repealed. (Specifically, these laws are the Thomas Amendment to the Agricultural Adjustment Act of May 12, 1933, and Public Resolution No. 10 of June 5, 1933.)

2. The Secretary of the Treasury should be authorized and directed to coin gold and to issue gold coins in suitable multiples of the existing definition of the gold dollar; that is, multiples of fifteen and five twenty-firsts grains of gold, nine-tenths fine. Such

— 173 —

coins should be full legal tender when not below a suitable limit of tolerance for the single piece, and when below that limit, should be legal tender in proportion to the actual weight.

3. All discretionary authority of the Secretary of the Treasury with respect to the issuance and circulation of gold certificates, or the purchase and sale of gold bullion at other than the statutory price, should be repealed.

4. The Secretary of the Treasury should be authorized and directed to issue gold certificates against any gold held in the Treasury not otherwise encumbered, and in exchange for any gold coin or gold bullion deposited with the Treasury. These gold certificates, when so issued, should be full legal tender.

5. The Secretary of the Treasury should be authorized and directed to redeem upon demand, in gold coin or gold certificates, at the option of the holder, any coins or currencies issued by the Treasury of the United States.

6. Each Federal Reserve bank should be required to redeem upon demand, in gold coin or gold certificates at the option of the holder, its Federal Reserve notes.

7. The Silver Purchase Act of 1934 should be amended so as to give the Secretary of the Treasury discretionary authority to buy or sell silver at market price, and to issue silver certificates or coin silver for the bullion purchased, at the rate of one silver dollar certificate for each silver dollar of 412½ grains of silver, nine-tenths fine. The silver dollars already issued, or which shall be issued, should be legal tender.

8. Federal Reserve notes issued in the manner prescribed by the Federal Reserve Act, as amended, should be designated receivable by the Treasury of the United States, by all Federal Reserve banks, and by all national banking associations in all payments whatsoever.

9. The Federal Reserve Act should be amended in such a way as to describe specifically, and in detail, the manner in which the Treasury shall hold and report the funds provided in law for the redemption and retirement of national bank notes, Federal Reserve notes and Federal Reserve bank notes, and the reserve fund held by the Treasury against deposits held in the Postal Savings Banks, so as to clearly separate these funds from

the General Fund of the Treasury.

10. The Gold Reserve Act of 1934 should be amended so as to require all national bank notes, Federal Reserve bank notes, Treasury notes of 1890, and United States notes, when received by any Federal Reserve bank, to be presented to the Treasury for payment and after payment to be destroyed.

11. The Gold Reserve Act of 1934 should be amended so as to specify that the words "lawful money" for reserves in the Federal Reserve banks, and for all other purposes concerning which the term "lawful money" is used in federal statute, shall mean all Treasury currency not in process of retirement; that is to say, gold coin, gold certificates, silver coin, silver certificates, and minor coin. Notes in process of retirement should not be used as reserves against deposits in Federal Reserve banks.

12. Section 16, paragraph 3, of the Federal Reserve Act should be amended to require reserves against both Federal Reserve notes in actual circulation, and reserves against deposits in Federal Reserve banks, in terms of lawful money as defined above.

13. Silver coins of denominations smaller than one dollar should be made legal tender only to the extent of, say, ten dollars in one payment.

14. Minor coins should be made legal tender only to the extent of, say, twenty-five or fifty cents in one payment.

The reader will readily recognize that the specific conditions described in these recommendations would have the effect of adopting a full gold coin standard in th United States. In the opinion of the author, it is the best method of removing the inconsistencies in our present monetary and banking structure.

It is scarcely surprising that whatever legislative attention has been bestowed upon the legal qualities of money since the war is the result of efforts exerted by the traditionalist, orthodox economists. Those who are primarily interested in the money flow are interested, to be blunt, only in the quantity of money and its velocity. They appear to be completely indifferent to its quality, whether legal or economic.

Many of the recommendations listed above have appeared in the gold standard bills introduced into Congress by such men as

Representative Howard Buffett of Nebraska, Representative Robert Hale of Maine, Representative Daniel Reed of New York, Representative Carroll Reece of Tennessee, Senator Styles Bridges of New Hampshire, and Representative Carl Hiestand of California. Perhaps the fact that a Democratic President was responsible for the abandonment of the gold standard domestically has contributed to the difficulty of restoring it, although there are many members of the Democratic Party who are aware of the shortcomings and inconsistencies of the present situation. One can only hope that blind partisanship can be subordinated to the requirements of all.

One obstacle to the adoption of the gold coin standard has been removed by the passage of time. In the more or less free gold markets of the world there is at present little, if any, premium on gold over the existing statutory price of $35.00 an ounce. The fear that some citizens might gain by selling gold in foreign markets if redemption of dollars in gold was restored is no longer valid. It is probable that it never was warranted, and the orthodox and traditionalist view has come to pass simply by the fall of the price of gold in these markets. This is precisely what the traditionalist had been saying all along.

The rather vague corollary fear that, somehow, citizens would immediately demand gold, cause a run on the Treasury, and generally behave like a small boy turned loose in a candy kitchen has never been removed. This fear is implicit in the argument that there is "not enough gold to go around." The fall in gold prices all over the world should have injected some suspicion of the wisdom of this fear, too. Apparently it has not.

It would be possible, of course, to adopt a gold bullion standard which, although having certain advantages over an inconvertible paper standard, would also have certain disadvantages. Perhaps, on the other hand, it might be adopted temporarily until such time as partisan fires had burned down sufficiently to take the next step toward redemption. At present it would involve little change from existing practices, yet would provide a road block to the future deterioration of our currency. Although the road block would not be impassable, it would slow down, at least, the momentum of our drive toward inconvertible paper money and the ultimate repudiation of the currency.

If a gold bullion standard were to be adopted, the following recommendations would remove, in the opinion of the author, the existing inconsistencies:

1. Repeal the laws making all coins and currencies of the United States full legal tender.

2. Repeal the discretionary authority of the Secretary of the Treasury to issue gold certificates and authorize and direct him to exchange for gold certificates, upon demand, any coins or currencies issued by the Treasury of the United States.

3. Each Federal Reserve bank should be required to redeem its Federal Reserve notes in gold certificates upon demand.

4. The Silver Purchase Act of 1934 should be amended so as to give the Secretary of the Treasury discretionary authority to buy or sell silver at market price, and to issue silver certificates or coin silver for the bullion purchased, at the rate of one silver dollar certificate for each silver dollar of 412½ grains, nine-tenths fine. There is no reason why the silver certificates and silver dollars should not be legal tender.

5. Federal Reserve notes issued in the manner prescribed by the Federal Reserve Act, as amended, should be made receivable by the Treasury, and by the Federal Reserve banks, in all payments whatsoever.

6. The Federal Reserve Act should be amended in such a way as to prescribe specifically, and in detail, the manner in which the Treasury shall hold and report the funds provided in law for the redemption and retirement of national bank notes, Federal Reserve notes and Federal Reserve bank notes, and the reserve fund held by the Treasury against deposits in the Postal Savings Banks, so as to separate these funds from the General Fund of the Treasury.

7. The Gold Reserve Act of 1934 should be amended so as to specify that the words "lawful money" for reserves in the Federal Reserve banks, and for all other purposes concerning which the term "lawful money" is used in federal statute, shall mean all Treasury currency not in process of retirement—gold certificates, silver coin, silver certificates, and minor coin. Notes in process of retirement should not be permitted to count as

reserves against deposits in Federal Reserve banks.

8. The Gold Reserve Act of 1934 should be amended so as to require that all national bank notes, Treasury notes of 1890, and United States notes, when reecived by any Federal Reserve bank, shall be presented to the Treasury for payment, and after payment shall be destroyed.

9. Section 16, paragraph 3, of the Federal Reserve Act should be amended to require reserves against both Federal Reserve notes in actual circulation, and reserves against deposits in the Federal Reserve banks, in lawful money as defined above.

10. Silver coins of denominations smaller than one dollar should be made legal tender only to the extent of, say, ten dollars in one payment.

11. Minor coins should be made legal tender only to the extent of, say, twenty-five or fifty cents in one payment.

To permit redemption of other money into gold by the process of authorizing the sale of gold bars of specified weight and fineness would provide, when added to the above, a consistent gold bullion standard which preserves the essence of the existing monetary structure yet guards against the dangers of a full paper money standard.

TABLE OF CASES CITED

McCulloch v. Maryland, 4 Wheat. 316 (1819).

M'Eowen v. Rose, 5 N.J. Law 582 (1819).

MacLeod v. Hoover, 159 La. 244; 105 So. 305 (1925).

Martin v. Bott, 46 N.E. (Ind.) 151 (1897).

Norman v. Baltimore and Ohio Railroad Co., 294 U.S. 240 (1935).

Nortz v. United States, 294 U.S. 317 (1935).

OK Bakery Company v. Morten Milling Company, 141 S.W. (Tex.) 436 (1940).

Ontario Bank v. Lightbody, 13 Wend. (N.Y.) 101 (1834).

Parrish v. Kohler, 11 Phila. (Pa.) 346 (1876).

Perry v. United States, 294 U.S. 330 (1935).

Polglass v. Olivier, 2 C. & J. Rep. 15 (1831).

Pryor v. Commonwealth of Kentucky, 2 Dana (Ky.) 298 (1834).

Railey et al. v. Bacon et al., 26 Miss. 455 (1853).

Rhodes v. O'Farrell, 2 Nev. 60 (1866).

Schoenberger v. Watts, 10 Am. Law Reg. (Pa.) 553 (1862).

State v. Boomer, 103 Iowa 106; 72 N.W. 424 (1897).

State v. Elliott, 202 Pac. (Kan.) 847 (1921).

State v. Finnegan, 127 Iowa 286 (1935).

State v. Neilon, 43 Ore. 168; 73 Pac. 321 (1903).

Thompson v. Butler, 95 U.S. 694 (1877).

Thorington v. Smith, 75 U.S. 1 (1869).

Thorndike v. United States, 2 Mason 1 (1819).

Tiley v. Courtier, 2 C. & J. 16 (1817).

Trebilcock v. Wilson, 12 Wall. 687 (1871).

United States v. Erie Railway Co., 106 U.S. 327 (1882).

United States v. Lissner, 12 Fed. Rep. 840 (1882).

United States v. Robertson, 5 Peters 641 (1831).

Veazie Bank v. Fenno, 8 Wall. 533 (1869).

Wade's Case, 5 Coke's Reports 114 (1601).

Ward v. Smith, 7 Wall. 447 (1868).

Warinbold v. Schlicting, 16 Iowa 243 (1864).

Wharton et al. v. Morris et al., 1 Dall. 124 (1785).

Whetstone v. Colley, 36 Ill. 328 (1865).

Wise Brothers v. Rogers, 24 Gratt. (Va.) 169 (1873).

Woodruff v. Trapnall, 51 U.S. 190 (1850).

Wright v. Reed, 3 T. R. 554 (1790).